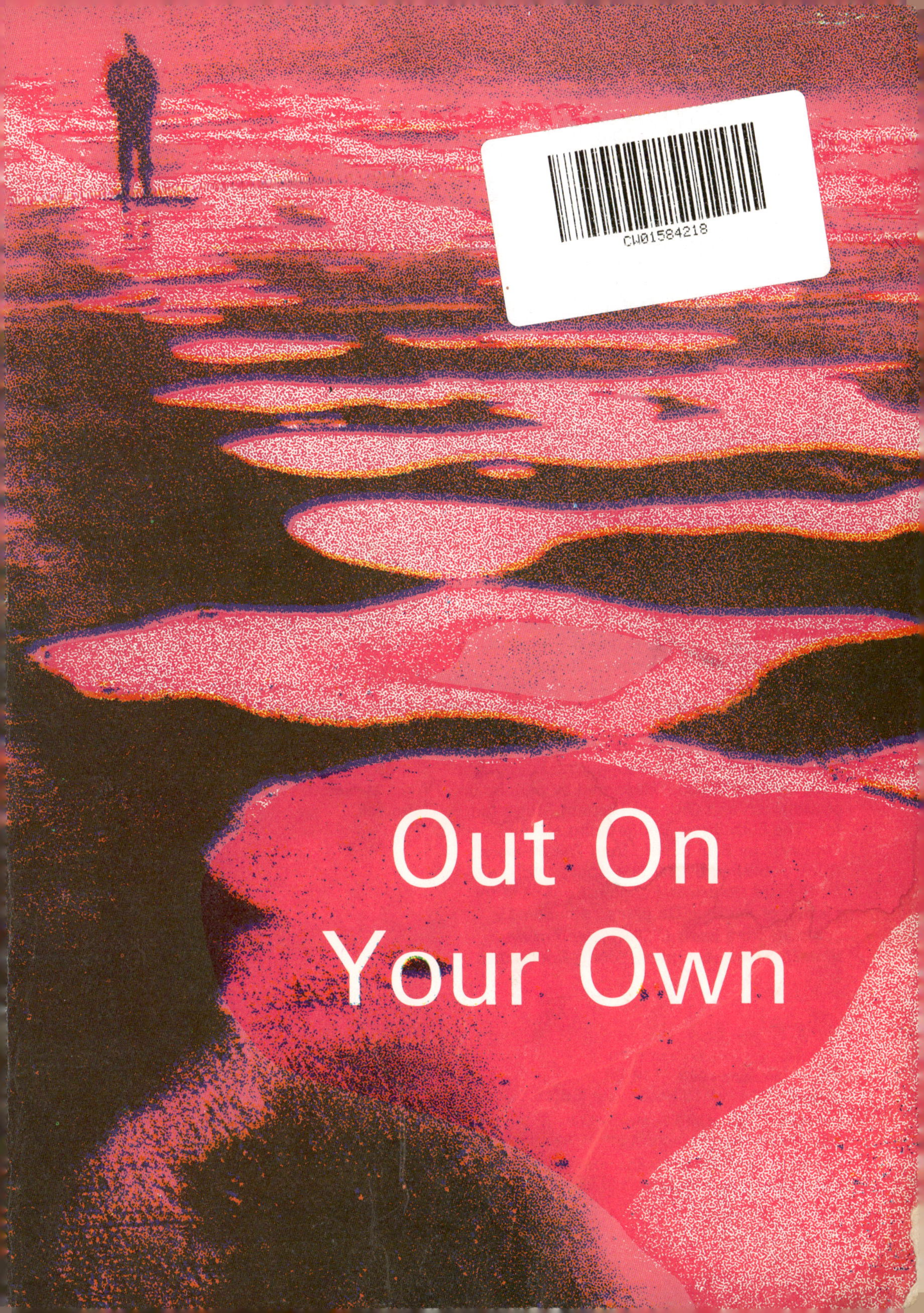

Out On Your Own

Acknowledgements

Grateful acknowledgement is made to the following for permission to use copyright material:

Atheneum Publishers, Inc. for the adaptation of "The Cave" by Jean McCord. Copyright © 1968 by Jean McCord from *Deep Where the Octopi Lie.* Used by permission of Atheneum Publishers, Inc./Ballena Press for "The Lone Woman of San Nicolas Island" by George Nidever. Adapted from *Original Accounts of the Lone Woman of San Nicolas Island,* with permission of Ballena Press, P.O. Box 711, Ramona, California 92065/The Bodley Head for "On the Cay" from *The Cay* by Theodore Taylor, published by The Bodley Head/Brandt & Brandt for "The Sea Devil" by Arthur Gordon. First published by *The Saturday Evening Post.* Copyright 1953, by Curtis Publishing Company. Reprinted by permission of Brandt & Brandt/John Ciardi for "Gulls Land and Cease To Be" from *Person to Person* by John Ciardi. Copyright 1964 by Rutgers, The State University. Reprinted by permission of the author/Curtis Brown, Ltd for "Amaroq, Farewell" from *Julie of the Wolves* by Jean Craighead George. Reprinted by permission of Curtis Brown, Ltd. Copyright © 1972 by Jean Craighead George/ McIntosh and Otis, Inc. for "Two Vipers" by Sally Watson, published in *Other Sandals,* 1966. Published by The Viking Press. Copyright 1966 by Sally Watson. Reprinted by permission of McIntosh and Otis, Inc./Pattern Music Ltd for "The 59th Street Bridge Song (Feelin' Groovy)" by Paul Simon, from *The Poetry of Rock,* published by Bantam Books, Inc., edited by Richard Goldstein/Penguin Books Ltd for "Island of the Blue Dolphins", Chapter 15 complete from Scott O'Dell: *Island of the Blue Dolphins* (Longman Young Books, 1961; Puffin Books, 1966). Copyright © 1960 by Scott O'Dell. Also for "On a Bicycle" from *Yevgeny Yevtushenko: Selected Poems,* translated by Robin Milner-Gulland and Peter Levi, S. J. (Penguin Modern European Poets, 1962), pp. 61–63. Copyright © Robin Milner-Gulland and Peter Levi, 1962/Mrs Celia Randall for the poem "Boy into Heron" from *My Kind of Verse.* Used by permission of the author.

Every effort has been made to obtain permission for copyright material and the publishers would be grateful for any discrepancies to be notified.

Editorial consultants
James Britton/Diana Bentley/Fran Oliver/Pat Parsons/Betty Root/Anne Rogers.

Editorial consultants (American Edition)
Theodore Clymer/Doris Gates/Marion L'Amoreaux/Helen Wardeburg

Level 13 artists
Don Albright/Victor Ambrus/Val Biro/Mike Cassaro/Tom Cooke/Diane and Leo Dillon/ Louise Emmons/Robert Geary/Judy Sue Goodwin/Tony Heald/Bill Hofmann/Lin Jenkins/Renate Kalkofen/Joan Paley/ Marianne Perlak/George Price/Alice and Martin Provensen/Tom Sgouros/Caroline Sharpe/Graham Smith/George Ulrich/Cecile Webster/Gareth Williams/Ed Young/Jon Zahourek.

Third impression 1980 118008
Reading 360 Level 13 Readers set ISBN 0 602 23104 3

Published by Ginn and Company Ltd
Elsinore House, Buckingham Street, Aylesbury, Bucks HP20 2NQ

Printed in Great Britain by Ebenezer Baylis & Son Ltd
The Trinity Press, Worcester, and London

Contents

Amaroq, Farewell

Lost on the Alaskan tundra, Miyax, an Eskimo girl, meets and becomes the companion of a pack of wolves—Amaroq, Silver, Nails and Kapu. Miyax is running from a troubled home situation to the promised pink room of a house in San Francisco where her pen friend Amy lives. But the wolves and memories of the words of her father, Kapugen, help Miyax to realize where her real home is.

Aha, ahahahahahaha! Miyax sat up, wondering what that was. Creeping halfway out of her bag, she peered into the sky to see a great brown bird manoeuvre its wings and speed west.

"A skua!" She was closer to the ocean than she thought, for the skua is a bird of the coastal waters of the Arctic. As her eyes followed it, they came to rest on an oil drum, the signpost of American civilization in the North. How excited she would have been to see this a month ago; now she was not so sure. She had her ulo and needles, her sled and her tent, and the world of her ancestors. And she liked the simplicity of that world. It was easy to understand. Out here she understood how she fitted into the scheme of the moon and stars and the constant rise and fall of life on the earth. Even the snow was part of her; she melted it and drank it.

Amaroq barked. He sounded as if he was no more than half a kilometre away.

"*Ow, ooo,*" she called. Nails answered, and then the whole pack howled briefly.

"I'm over here!" she shouted joyously, jumping up and down. "Here by the lake." She paused. "You know that. You know everything about me all the time."

The wind began to rise as the sun started back to the horizon. The lake responded with a boom that sounded like a pistol shot. The freeze was deepening. Miyax lit a fire and put on her pot. A warm stew would taste good and the smoke and flames would make the tundra home.

Presently Amaroq barked forcefully, and the pack answered. Then the royal voice sounded from another position, and Silver checked in from across the lake. Nails gave a warning snarl and the pups whispered in "woofs".

Miyax shaded her eyes; her wolves were barking from points around a huge circle and she was in the middle. This was strange—they almost always stayed together. Suddenly Amaroq barked ferociously, his voice angry and authoritative. Silver yelped, then Nails and Kapu. They had something at bay.

She stepped onto the lake and skipped towards them. Halfway across she saw a dark head rise above the hill, and a beast with a head as large as the moon rose to its hind feet, massive paws swinging.

"Grizzly!" she gasped and stopped stone-still, as the huge animal rushed onto the ice. Amaroq and Nails leapt at its face and sprang away before the bear could strike. They were heading it off, trying to prevent it from crossing. The bear snarled, lunged forward and galloped towards Miyax.

She ran towards her tent. The wind was in her face and she realized that she was downwind of the bear, her scent blowing right to him. She darted off in another direction, for bears have poor eyesight and cannot track if they can-

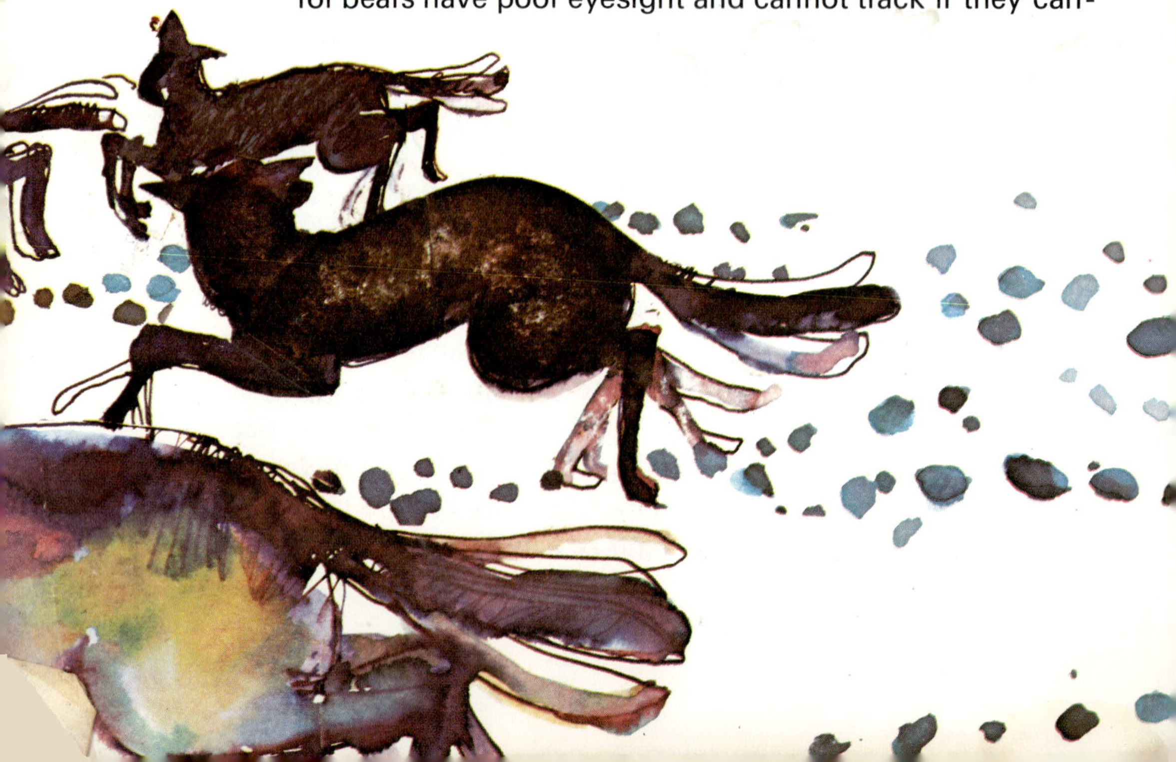

not smell. Slipping and sliding, she reached the south bank as the grizzly staggered forward, then crumpled to its knees and sat down. She wondered why he was not in hibernation. The wolves had been sleeping all day—they could not have wakened the bear. She sniffed the air to try to smell the cause, but only odourless ice crystals stung her nose.

The pack kept harassing the sleepy beast, barking and snarling, but with no intention of killing it. They were simply trying to drive it away—away from her, she realized.

Slowly the bear got to its feet and permitted itself to be herded up the lake bank and back to where it had come from. Reluctantly, blindly, it staggered before the wolves. Occasionally it stood up like a giant, but mostly it roared in the agony of sleepiness.

Yapping, barking, darting, the wolves drove the grizzly far out on the tundra. Finally they veered away and, breaking into a joyous gallop, dashed over the snow and out of sight. Their duty done, they were running—not to hunt, not to kill—but simply for fun.

Miyax was trembling. She had not realized the size and ferocity of the dark bear of the North, who is called "grizzly" inland, and "brown bear" along the coasts—*Ursus arctos*. Large ones, like the grizzly her wolves had driven away, weighed over five hundred kilograms and stood nearly three metres tall when they reared. Miyax wiped a bead of perspiration from her forehead. Had he come upon her tent, with one curious sweep of his paw he would have snuffed out her life while she slept.

"Amaroq, Nails, Kapu," she called. "I thank you. I thank you."

As she packed to travel on, she thought about her escorts. Wolves did not like civilization. Where they had once dwelt all over North America they now lived in remote parts of Canada, in only two of the lower forty-eight states and in the wilderness of Alaska. Even the roadless North Slope had fewer wolves than it did before the gussaks erected their military bases and brought aeroplanes, snow-mobiles, electricity and jeeps to the Arctic.

As she thought about the gussaks she suddenly knew why the brown bear was awake. The Americans' hunting season had begun! Her wolves were in danger! The gussaks were paid to shoot them. A man who brought in the left ear of a wolf to the warden was rewarded with a large bounty. The bounty was evil to the old men at the seal camp, for it encouraged killing for money, rather than need. Kapugen considered the bounty the gussaks' way of deciding that the amaroqs could not live on this earth any-more. "And no men have that right," he would say. "When the wolves are gone there will be too many caribou grazing the grass and the lemmings will starve. Without the lem-mings the foxes and birds and weasels will die. Their passing will end smaller lives upon which even man depends, whether he knows it or not, and the top of the world will pass into silence."

Miyax was worried. The oil drum she had seen when the skua flew over marked the beginning of civilization and the end of the wilderness. She must warn her pack of the danger ahead. She had learned to say many things to them; but now, the most important of all, the ear-twist or bark that would turn them back, she did not know.

How, she thought, do I shout "Go away! Go far, far away!" She sang:

Go away, royal wolf,
Go away, do not follow.
I'm a gun at your head,
When I pass the oil drum.

Threads of clouds spun up from the earth and trailed across the tundra. They marked the beginning of a white-out. Miyax changed her plans to travel that night, crept into her shelter and watched the air turn white as the snow arose from the ground and hung all around her. She closed her tent flap and took out her pot. In it she put a piece of fat from the bladder-bag and a scrap of sinew. She lit the sinew and a flame illuminated her tiny home. She took out the comb.

As she carved she saw that it was not a comb at all, but Amaroq. The teeth were his legs, the handle his head. He was waiting to be released from the bone. Surprised to see him, she carved carefully for hours and finally she let him out. His neck was arched, his head and tail were lifted. Even his ears had a message. "I love you," they said.

A bird called faintly in the darkness. Miyax wondered what kind it was and what it was doing so far north at this date. Too sleepy to think, she unlaced her boots, undressed and folded her clothes. The bird called from the edge of her sleeping skin. Holding her candle above her head, she crept towards the door and peered into the bright eyes of a golden plover. He was young, for he wore the splotched plumage of the juvenile and still had a trace of baby-yellow around his beak. He slumped against her skins.

Gently she slipped her hand under his feet, picked him up and brought him close to her. His black and gold feathers gleamed in the spluttering light. She had never beheld a plover so closely and now understood why Kapugen had called them "the spirit of the birds". The plover's golden eye and red noseband made it look like one of the dancers in the Bladder Feast.

"You are lost," she said. "You should be far from here. Perhaps in Labrador. Perhaps even in your winter home on the plains of Argentina. And so you are dying. You need insects and meat. But I'm so glad you're here." Then she added, "I shall call you Tornait, the bird spirit."

She eased the bird inside her warm sleeping skin, cut off a small piece of caribou meat and held it out. Tornait ate it ravenously, then rested. She fed him once more, and then he tucked his head in his back feathers and went to sleep.

The following night the white-out was still so dense that Miyax could not see the ground when she crept out for snow to melt and drink.

"I won't go on tonight," she said to Tornait when she came inside. "But I do not care. I have food, light, furs, fire and a pretty companion." That evening she polished her carving of Amaroq and talked to Tornait. The plover was incredibly tame, perhaps because he lived in the most barren parts of the world where there were no men, perhaps because he was lonely. Tornait ran over her skins, flitted to her head and shoulders and sang when she sang.

On the next afternoon the white-out was but a frosty mist. Miyax was cooking dinner when Tornait drew his feathers to his body and stood up in alarm. She listened for a long time before she heard the snow scream as footsteps pressed it. Scrambling to the door, she saw Kapu in the mist, frost on his whiskers.

"Hi!" she called. He did not turn round for he was looking at something in the distance. Presently Amaroq swept into view and stopped beside him.

"Amaroq!" she shouted. "Amaroq, how are you?" Tossing her head in wolf happiness, she crawled out of her tent on all fours and nudged him under the chin. He arched his neck grandly. Then, with a glance at Kapu, he ran out onto the lake. The young wolf followed and, laughing joyously, Miyax crawled after them both. She had not gone far before Amaroq stopped and glared at her. She stayed where she was. The regal pair leapt away, snow billowing up from their strides like smoke.

Getting to her knees she looked for Silver, Nails and the other pups, but they did not follow the pair. Miyax rocked back on her heels. Could it be that the leader of the pack was teaching the leader of the pups? She nodded slowly as she comprehended. Of course. To be a leader required not only fearlessness and intelligence, but experience and schooling. The head of a wolf pack needed to be trained, and who better to do this than Amaroq?

"And I know what you'll teach," she called out. "You'll teach him which animals to harvest. You'll teach him to make all decisions. You'll teach him how to close in on a caribou, and where to bed the wolf pack down; and you'll teach him to love and protect."

The white-out vanished, the stars blazed out and San Francisco called to Miyax. It was time to move on. Kapu

was now at school.

"But how shall I tell them not to follow me anymore?" she asked Tornait as she crawled back into her tent.

"Of course!" she gasped. She had been told by Amaroq himself how to say "stay back" when he had wanted Kapu alone. He had walked forward, turned round and glared into her eyes. She had stopped in her tracks and gone home. Eagerly she practised. She ran forward, looked over her shoulder and glared. "Stay, Amaroq. Stay where you are!"

Humming to herself she took down her tent, rolled it into a bundle and threw it onto the new sled. Then she stuffed her pack and tucked Tornait into the hood of her parka. Sticking her toes into her snowshoes, she took a bearing on the constant star. The snow squeaked under her feet, and for the first time she felt the dry bite of the cold right through her parka and boots. To her this meant the temperature was zero, the point every year when she began to feel chilly. Dancing and swinging her arms to get warm, she picked up the thongs of her sled and walked towards the sea. The sled glided lightly behind her.

She did not hear the aeroplane; she saw it. The low sun of noon struck its aluminium body and it sparkled like a star in the sky. It was a small plane, the type bush pilots use to carry people over the roadless tundra and across the rugged mountains of Alaska where cars cannot go. Presently its sound reached her ears and the throb of the engine reminded her that this was the beginning of the season when bush pilots took the gussaks out to hunt. The craft tipped its wings and zigzagged across the sky. When it continued to zag she realized the pilot was following a meandering river where game wintered. A river, she thought; rivers led to the sea. I am nearing the end of my journey; Point Hope might be but one sleep away. She

quickened her pace.

The aeroplane banked, turned and came towards her. It seemed as big as an eagle as it skimmed low over the ground. Bright flashes of fire burst from its side.

"They *are* hunting," she said to Tornait. "Let's get in the oil drum. I look like a bear in these clothes."

Just before she reached the drum she crossed the footsteps of Amaroq and Kapu. They had passed this way only moments ago, for the snow crystals their warm feet had melted were not yet frozen again. The plane continued to come towards her. Apparently she had been seen. She kicked snow over her sled and pack and crawled to the front of the barrel. It was sealed. She could not get inside. Scurrying to the other end she found that it, too, was closed. Desperately she threw herself under the curve of the drum and lay still. Much of her was still exposed. Flailing her hands and feet, she stirred up the light snow. It arose like a cloud and settled upon her as the plane soared above.

Shots rang out. The plane roared away and Miyax opened her eyes. She was still alive and the air hunters

were over the river. The plane banked and flew back, this time very low. Tornait struggled.

"Be still," she said. The gunfire snapped again and, eyes wide open, she saw that it was not aimed at her.

"Amaroq!" Horrified, she watched him leap into the air as a splatter of shots burst beside him. Digging in his claws, he veered to the right and left as Kapu ran to join him. Teeth bared, angrily growling, Amaroq told him to go. Kapu sped off. The plane hesitated, then pursued Amaroq.

Shots hit the snow in front of him. He reared and turned.

"Amaroq!" she screamed. "Here! Come here!"

The plane swerved, dived and skimmed about nine metres above the ground. Its guns blasted. Amaroq stumbled, pressed back his ears and galloped across the tundra like a shooting star. Then he reared and dropped on the snow.

He was dead.

"For a bounty," she screamed. "For money, the magnificent Amaroq is dead!" Her throat constricted with grief, and sobs choked her.

The plane banked and came back. Kapu was running to Amaroq. His ears were pressed to his head and his legs moved so swiftly they were a blur. Bullets showered the snow around him. He leapt, dodged and headed for the oil drum. His wide eyes and open mouth told Miyax he was afraid for the first time in his life. Blindly he ran, and as he came by she reached out and tripped him. He sprawled across the snow and lay still. While the plane coasted off to make another turn, she covered Kapu with flakes.

The snow turned red with blood from his shoulder. Miyax rolled under the barrel.

The air exploded and she stared up into the belly of the plane. Bolts, doors, wheels, red, white, silver and black, the plane flashed before her eyes. In that instant she saw great cities, bridges, radios, schoolbooks. She saw the pink room, long highways, TV sets, telephones and electric lights. Black exhaust enveloped her, and civilization became this monster that snarled across the sky.

The plane shrank before her eyes, then turned and grew big again. Tornait flew to the top of the barrel, screaming his alarm cry and beating his wings.

Kapu tried to get up.

"Don't move," Miyax whispered. "They're coming for Amaroq." Knowing Kapu did not understand, she reached out and softly stroked him, singing: "Lie still. Lie still." She watched him slump back in the snow without a sound.

The plane returned at so low a level that she could see the men in the cockpit; their coat collars pulled up around their necks, their crash helmets and goggles gleaming. They were laughing and watching the ground. Desperately Miyax thought about Silver, Nails and the pups. Where were they? They must be clear targets on the white snow. Maybe not—they were light in colour, not black.

Suddenly the engine accelerated, the wing flaps pressed down and the craft climbed, banked and sailed down the river like a migrating bird. It did not turn round.

Miyax buried her fingers in Kapu's fur. "They did not

even stop to get him!" she cried. "They did not even kill him for money. I don't understand. I don't understand. *Ta vun ga vun ga,*" she cried. "*Pisupa gasu punga.*" She spoke of her sadness in Eskimo, for she could not recall any English.

Kapu's blood spread like fish ripples on the snow. She wriggled to him and clamped her thumb on the vein that was gushing. She held the pressure—a minute, an hour—she did not know how long. Then Tornait called hungrily. Cautiously she lifted her hand. The bleeding had stopped.

"*Ta gasu,*" she said to Kapu. She brushed the snow off her sled and took out her poles. She set up her tent beside the barrel, banked the snow round the bottom to seal out the wind and spread her ground cloth under it. When she tried to push Kapu into the shelter she found him too heavy. He lifted his head, then dropped it wearily. Miyax decided to build the tent around him. She took everything down and started all over again.

This time she eased the ground skin under him bit by bit until he lay on the fur. Then she kicked the oil drum to free it from the ice, rolled it close to him and erected her tent against it. She sealed the gaps with snow.

The drum was old, for it had different markings from those around Barrow, but like them, it was barely rusted. The frigid winters and the dry desert-like conditions of the tundra prevent metals, papers and refuse from deteriorating as they do in warmer zones. In the Arctic, all artifacts

are preserved for ages. Even throwing them into the oceans does not work a change, for the water freezes round them, and as icebergs they come back onto the shores. The summer sun unveils them again.

Miyax melted snow, cut off meat for Tornait and fed him. He flew down from the barrel and ran into the tent. Hopping onto her furry sleeping skin, he puffed up his feathers, stood on one foot and went to sleep.

With the stew bubbling, Kapu resting and Tornait asleep, Miyax dared to think of Amaroq. She would go and bid him goodbye. She tried to get up, but she could not move. Grief held her in a vice-like clamp.

About an hour later Kapu lifted his head, rolled his eyes and accepted chunks of stew. Miyax petted his head and told him to lie still while she looked at his wound. It was long and deep and she knew it must be sewn together.

Taking a piece of sinew from the ground skin, she threaded it into her needle and pierced the soft flesh. Kapu growled.

"*Xo lur pajau, sexo,*" she sang soothingly. "*Lupir pajau se suri vanga pangmane majo riva pangmane.*" Monotonously repeating over and over the healing song of the old bent lady, she hypnotized Kapu as she closed the wound. The perspiration was running down her cheeks when she had finished, but she was able to tell him that he would get well and return to lead their pack.

The sun set in a navy blue sky, and the stars sparkled on

and off as they spoke of their vast distances from the earth. About midnight the inside of the tent began to glow green and Kapu's eyes shone like emeralds. Miyax peered out of the flap door. Fountains of green fire rose from the earth and shot to the top of the black velvet sky. Red and white lights sprayed out of the green. The northern lights were dancing. The lakes boomed, and Nails howled mournfully.

Miyax howled back to tell him where she was. Then Silver barked and the pups called too. Each voice sounded closer than the last; the pack was coming towards the oil drum as it searched for Amaroq and Kapu.

Miyax stepped into the light of the aurora. It was time to bid Amaroq farewell. She tried to go forward but her feet would not move. Grief still held them useless. Clutching her left knee in both hands, she lifted her foot and put it down; then she lifted the other and put it down, slowly making her way across the turquoise snow.

Amaroq lay where he had fallen, his fur shining in the strange magnetic light.

"Amaroq . . ." She took her carving from her pocket and got down on her knees. Singing softly in Eskimo, she told him she had no bladder for his spirit to dwell in, but that she had his totem. She asked him to enter the totem and be with her forever.

For a long time she held the carving over his body. Presently, the pain in her breast grew lighter and she knew the wolf was with her.

The stars had slipped down in the sky when at last she stood up and walked swiftly back to Kapu.

All night Miyax sat beside him and listened to Silver, Nails and the pups.

"Owwwwwww," they cried in a tone she had never heard before, and she knew they were crying for Amaroq.

Jean Craighead George

The Cave

"I know I'm to blame," the teller of this story says. Find out what happened and see whether you agree that Charley was guilty.

George has gone. He's either dead, or he's crawled off into one of the deep caves and laid himself down in darkness and silence to die. How long do you think it will take for an old man to die of a broken heart?

I know I'm to blame. I had my part in what happened, except right at the end when the gang went and did what they did. I wasn't in on that, but I might as well have been. It was the same in the end, anyway. When the work and the glory was gone, there was simply no reason for George to go on living.

I was the only one who knew about him at first.

One Saturday morning in early spring, I'd left the house for a run. I galloped long and hard along the banks of the Godalming River to get the kinks out of my knees.

I'd got a little further than I'd ever been before, when I'd suddenly seen a new path angling up from the river road.

I had swung into it and loped along uphill as far as I could until a stitch in my side made me stop. As I was looking up the hill about six metres, I saw something hidden behind some brush. I wish now I'd gone on and left it alone, but my curiosity always gets the better of me. I went soundlessly up the hill in my running shoes, noticing that there were no steps or tracks to give this away, whatever it was. I got up to it and found it was the mouth of a cave, high on the hill with a perfect view up and down the river. It had been boarded over with timber and some rough, river-washed planks. A skinny door hung slightly open on leather hinges.

I started to stick my nose in the crack when, just then, a voice remarked behind my back, "Looking for something?" and I spun around so fast and so guiltily that I almost lost my balance.

There was an old man sitting casually under a tree and keeping so still that I hadn't even seen him. But he had been watching me, probably since the moment that I'd started up the hill.

He looked so weird I recognized him right away for what he was, a tramp. Yet he wasn't like any other tramp I'd ever seen. His hair was long and tangled, falling almost to his shoulders like a Biblical prophet's, and his face was a mass of porcupine bristles, not having been shaved in weeks. His nose was a narrow, anxious-looking beak, but his brown eyes were as soft as the spring water, and his mouth was clamped on the broken stub of a pipe, unlit. There was that look in his eye that told me he was harmless.

"Sit down, boy, if you like." He motioned me over.

I went and squatted, looking up and down at the view companionably.

After a while he spoke again. "Got a name?"

I almost said, "Yes, sir, Charles," but I stopped myself. "Charley," I grunted.

"Good name," he said. "Long lineage; way back. You heard of Charlemagne?"

"Yes." I looked at him curiously. I'd studied that in history classes, but where had he heard about him?

"Same name. Means Charley the Greatest. A royal name. Dozens of crowned heads answered to it."

"Oh yeah?" I was interested in spite of myself. Now why hadn't the teacher mentioned that? It might have made that history lesson a little easier to take.

"Got a pretty royal name myself," the old tramp was saying. "George. Same as six kings of England, two of Greece, a president of the United States and a saint who was quite a dragon hunter. Not that it's ever brought me much." He was looking ruefully at his pipe, which was quite empty. And then to make it look funny and to make me laugh, which I did, he wriggled his big toe, which was sticking right out of the tip of one shoe. I wished I had some tobacco to give him, but I didn't. Maybe another time.

"You live in there?" I jerked my thumb at the boards hiding the cave.

"Well, let's just say it's my Passport to Paradise."

Ugh, I thought, this old boy's got a few bats flying round in his belfry. But he had my curiosity aroused again, just the same. I'll come back tomorrow and bring him some tobacco, I thought. I can take some from my dad and he'll never miss it.

As it happened, I didn't return the next day because my parents made me go with them to visit Aunt Margaret.

A week later, Saturday again, I wrapped some tobacco in a handkerchief and headed back to see old George. Usually I would have gone to the clubhouse and spent the

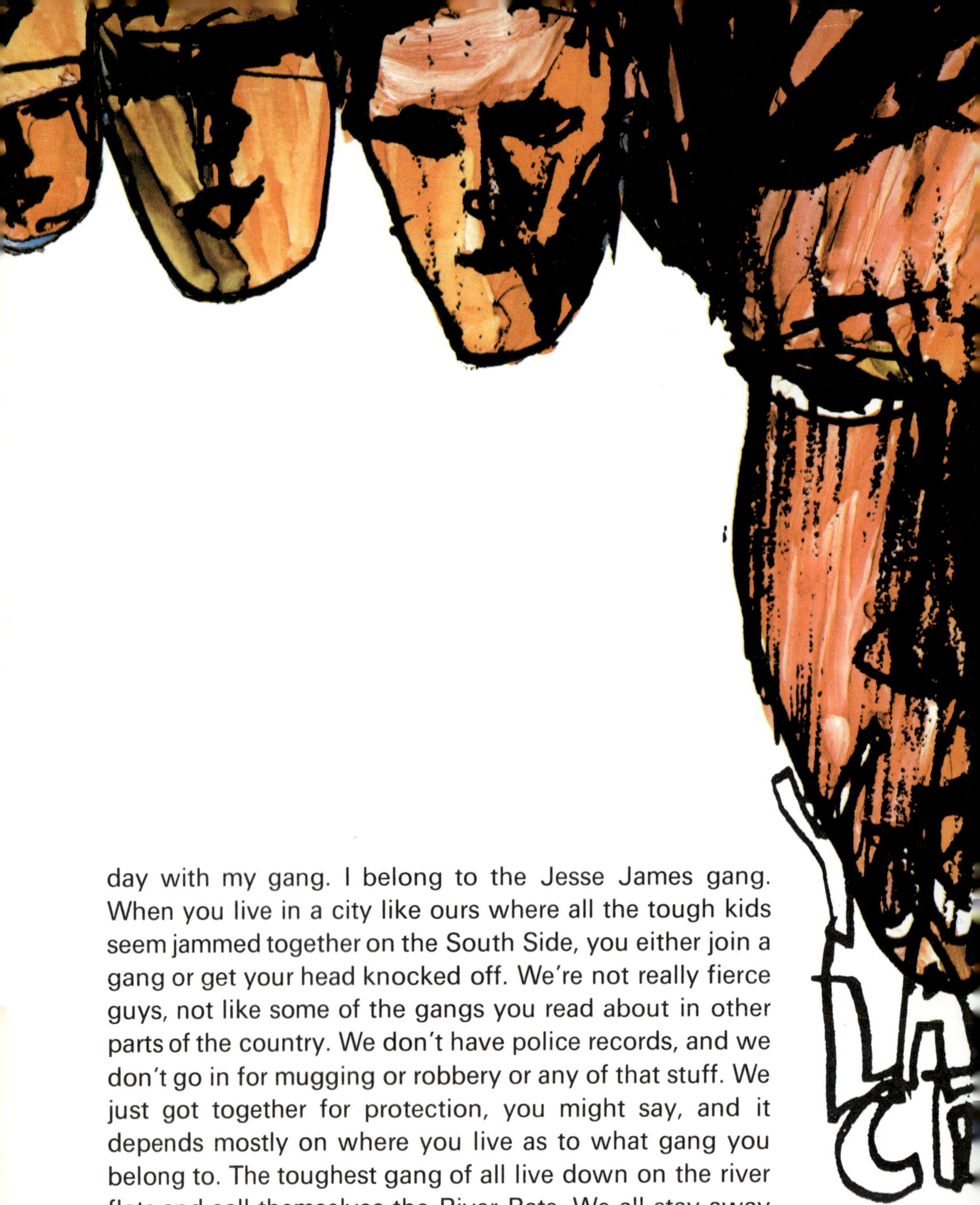

day with my gang. I belong to the Jesse James gang. When you live in a city like ours where all the tough kids seem jammed together on the South Side, you either join a gang or get your head knocked off. We're not really fierce guys, not like some of the gangs you read about in other parts of the country. We don't have police records, and we don't go in for mugging or robbery or any of that stuff. We just got together for protection, you might say, and it depends mostly on where you live as to what gang you belong to. The toughest gang of all live down on the river flats and call themselves the River Rats. We all stay away

from them, as much as we can. The River Rats are . . . well, I just wouldn't have wanted to belong to them, not then.

I was walking on the new trail leading to George's place, going slowly, when I felt a sudden prickle of cold air on my neck, and the coolness led me right to a small opening that slanted down into the ground. I knew it was the airhole for some cave, a new one, one I'd never been in. You see, the cliffs are made of limestone, and waters trickling down through them for millions of years have cut out many caves. For a long time now my gang's been looking for a cave, one we could keep secret for ourselves. We wanted to hold meetings there, safe from the other neighbourhood gangs, have initiations and just sit around in the darkness lit up by a warm fire and chat about things.

This was it. Our own cave! I would go and tell the gang about it.

I ran all the way back, and made about as good a time as was possible with only two legs.

The gang were all gathered at the usual place, an aban-

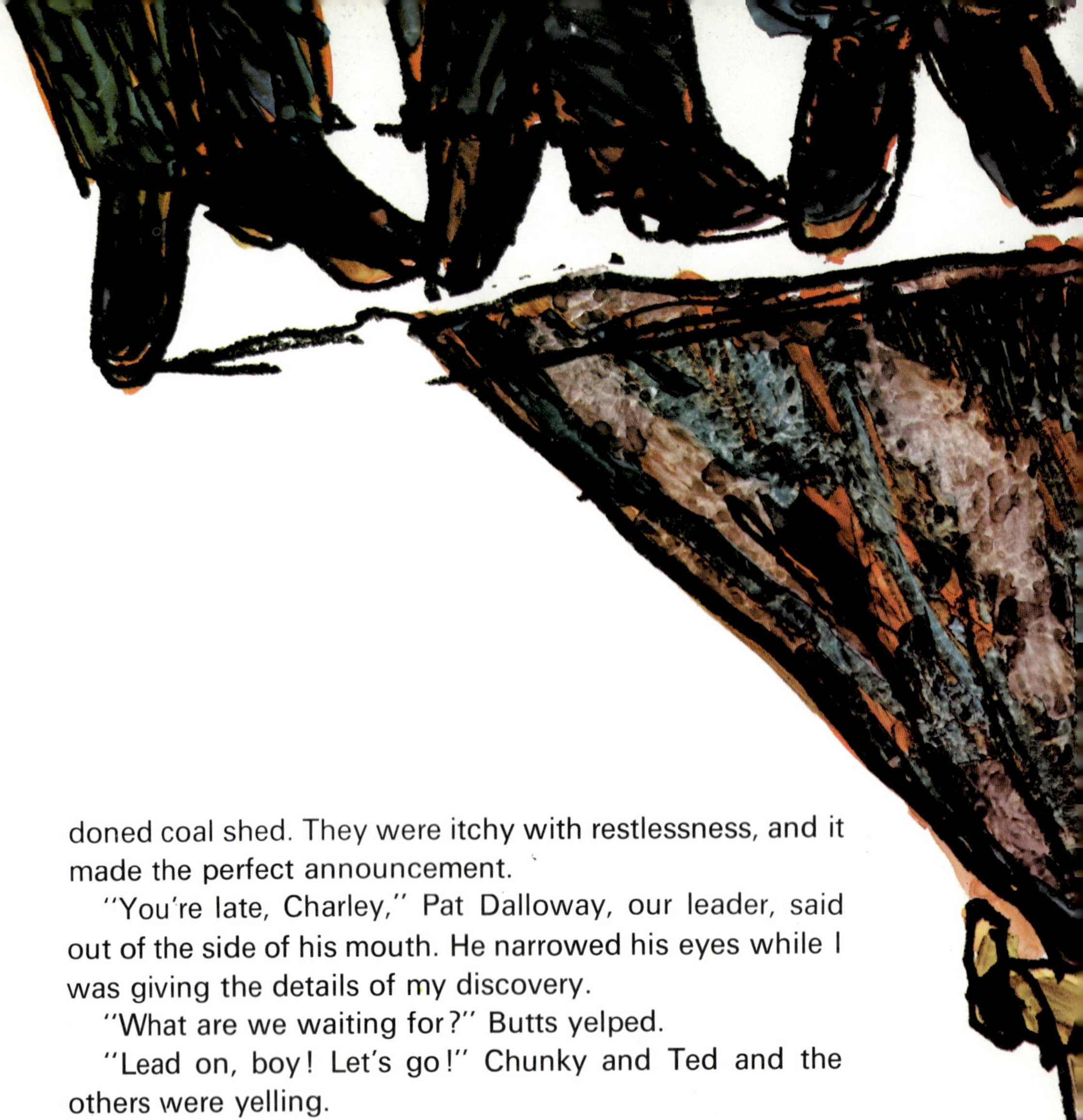

doned coal shed. They were itchy with restlessness, and it made the perfect announcement.

"You're late, Charley," Pat Dalloway, our leader, said out of the side of his mouth. He narrowed his eyes while I was giving the details of my discovery.

"What are we waiting for?" Butts yelped.

"Lead on, boy! Let's go!" Chunky and Ted and the others were yelling.

They followed me, a pounding troop at my heels, though we had to stop several times for Chunky to catch his breath.

We clustered round at the spot, and Pat fell on his knees and stuck his head into the hole. He pulled it out again quickly. "It's a good one, Charley," he said with a grin at the gang, "and since you were the finder, to you goes the honour."

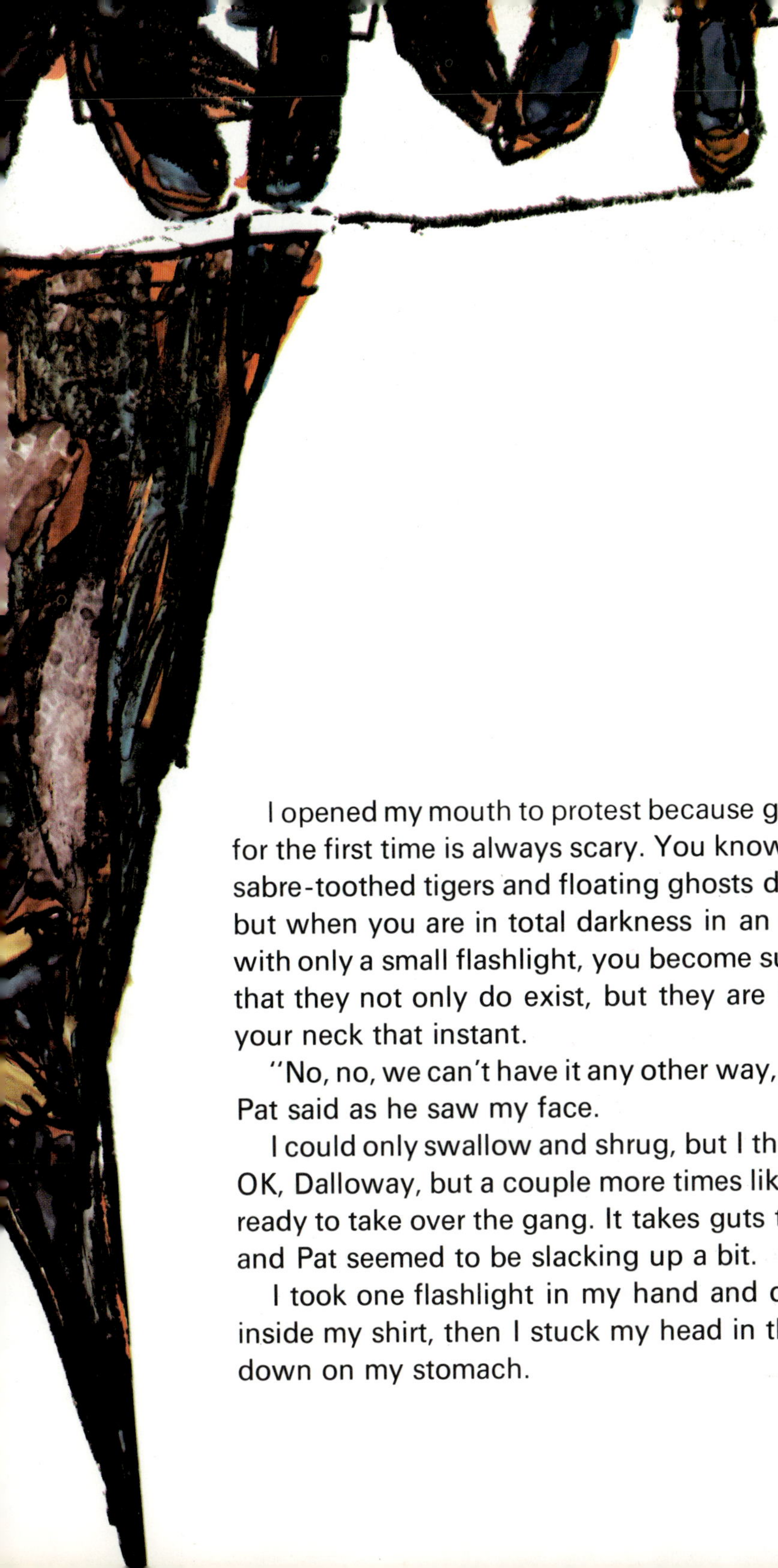

I opened my mouth to protest because going into a cave for the first time is always scary. You know such things as sabre-toothed tigers and floating ghosts don't really exist, but when you are in total darkness in an unknown place with only a small flashlight, you become suddenly positive that they not only do exist, but they are breathing down your neck that instant.

"No, no, we can't have it any other way, can we, boys?" Pat said as he saw my face.

I could only swallow and shrug, but I thought to myself, OK, Dalloway, but a couple more times like this and I'll be ready to take over the gang. It takes guts to be the leader, and Pat seemed to be slacking up a bit.

I took one flashlight in my hand and dropped another inside my shirt, then I stuck my head in the hole and laid down on my stomach.

After wriggling in till my feet were out of sight of the gang, this little hole took me by surprise and suddenly slanted down at a swift angle. There was nothing to grab at along the way, just the soft sandstone walls worn into smoothness by the ancient waters. I slid down the hole as if I was on one of those little tin slides at a children's playground, and I dropped down into what seemed the centre of the earth. When I'd given up hope, I rolled out of that chute like a marble and fell about a metre to bounce on soft, cool sand. The flashlight shot out of my hand, pointing away from me, its puny beam lost in the vastness of this black cavern. I sat there rubbing my hands and stomach to ease the smarting and feeling myself, but I was OK. However, the thought occurred to me before I even reached for the light, how was I going to get out? That hole was too steep and smooth to climb back up, and something told me the gang wasn't going to follow me in.

I crawled over to the flashlight. When I turned it up towards the ceiling, its beam just got lost in the blackness. There was no sound in the cave. It felt as if there had never been a single sound ever in there. I went over to the hole I'd dropped out of and listened up it for the gang. I couldn't hear them. It was so spooky in that huge cave that it felt as if I was down among the dead, like in the catacombs I'd read about, and I even looked around a bit, but not too much. I couldn't see anything, just creamy yellow walls and white sand underfoot. I wondered if I was the first person who had ever been in there. It certainly looked like it. There wasn't a mark on the walls, and I couldn't see any footprints. My light was wavering around, and I got a desolate feeling that it was going to go out on me.

I had to get out. I turned and started walking, hurrying for what seemed like a few kilometres, but there's nothing to judge by, so you don't really know how far. A few steps

even seemed like a long way. My flashlight was getting dimmer and my fear was growing. And just when my light was about to go out for good and I was going to throw myself down and yell in terror for help, I saw a paleness around a bend.

I shot round the corner and found myself in a room about as big as our living room at home. It was still a cave, but someone was living in it. A few scraps of furniture sat around, made-up furniture of boxes and planks and junk. The front of the cave was boarded over with old planks and a small door swung lazily on leather hinges.

I stopped right in the middle of it and looked around. And then I saw what was really so different from anyone's living room in a house. The walls were covered with statues. Not the kind carved from wood; these statues were cut right out of the walls in what our art teacher calls bas-relief. They seemed almost to be living beings who were growing out of the rock, and all of them were watching me carefully. I was so glad to see the sunlight through the door, I could only sob with relief. But as usual my curiosity was still with me, so I looked around. On one wall I could recognize certain figures. One was Lincoln; next to him was George Washington. Another wall held a Crucifixion scene and next to that was a man on a horse, both of them wearing armour, spearing a dragon who was lashing around with claws and scales all over him. They were all big, more than life-size, and you could see that somebody had put an awful lot of work into them.

As I walked towards the swinging door, it struck me then. I'd seen that door before. I stepped through it, looked around feeling terribly foolish and found myself staring right into George's startled eyes. I guess he'd never seen anyone walk out of his cave before.

"Hey!" he said.

"Yeah, I know." I waved my hand backwards. "I got lost." I grinned feebly. "A wicked witch changed me into a rabbit and a dog chased me down a hole, and well, here I am . . ."

It was the best I could do. I was so happy I wanted to run over and shake both his hands.

George looked at me for a minute, then he laughed. "You're all right, kid," he said. "I told you Charley was a lucky name. Come and sit down. You look pretty fagged out."

I stretched out beside him in the sun and squirmed with

the pure pleasure of it on my body. It was only when I rolled over on my stomach, wanting to hug the ground, that I felt the extra flashlight biting into me.

"What time is it?" I asked, my face against the dirt.

George squinted at the sun. "Mebbe two o'clock, or so."

I sighed. I'd been in the cave less than half an hour. It had seemed like days.

"That's pretty good stuff in there," I said cautiously. "It looks like . . . well . . . like a real art gallery."

George looked down at his hands. They were square and blocky with dirt under the nails. "It fills my time," he said. He stared at them for a long time. Finally, gazing down the river, he said quietly, "Look, Charley. I don't pay rent on that cave, but it's mine just the same. I found it first. I fixed it up. Been here over five years now, and I've got a lot more work to do. I'm just beginning to get good." He looked at me, and I could actually see the pleading in his eyes. "If people knew about me, they'd come and drive me out. Against the law, or if it isn't, they'd make one. Now why don't you just go on home and keep your mouth shut. Here. Take this." He handed me a little bit of wood that he had been working on when I'd stepped out of his home. It was a tiny carved fawn, its legs folded under itself and its head bent as though it was hiding from dogs who were hunting it.

"Well, thanks. Thanks a lot." I got up and stood there, tongue-tied. I wanted to say I was sorry I'd intruded, that it was to save my neck that I had to come out that way. But he must have known. After all, he knew that cave better than I did, and right then he was welcome to it, all of it. I had no intention of telling anyone, certainly not the gang; but I had to get back to them before they got up a search party for me.

I plunged down George's hill, and when I got to where I'd left the gang, I slowed down and sauntered up to them. They were all in a knot with serious looks on their faces, and when they turned round, their jaws dropped.

"You lily-livered chickens doing anything to get me out of there?" I blustered at them.

"Hey, Charley! Charley, old boy. We thought you were a goner, sure!" They were all shouting at once and pounding me on the back.

"You've been in there before, wise guy, haven't you?" Pat scowled at me. "Tried to be smart. Sneaked out another way and let us think you were lost." He was really mad.

What was I going to tell them to make them stay out of the cave? I had to think up a story, and a good one, quick. "Look," I said. "It's not even a cave. It's just a kind of tunnel, not big enough for a cat. It goes down a long way, straight, and then winds around and comes out behind the bend over there, somewhere. I didn't even mark it."

"You were gone too long," Pat said, shoving his face next to mine.

"I was scrabbling along on my belly the whole way. See?" I showed them the raw marks on my arms and stomach. "It never gets more than half a metre high or wide." I turned. "Come on. Let's go home. I'm starved."

"What have you got in your hand, Charley? You must have found something."

I stared at my own hand as if I'd never seen it before. I hadn't thought to put the little carving in my pocket. Then I did a stupid thing. Instead of bluffing my way out, I gave a leap downhill and started running hard. With a head start none of them could catch me, and I raced along as fast as I'd ever run in my life before. I could hear them for a while pounding along almost at my back, but one by one, I outran them and got to my home.

I sped up to my bedroom, and in a couple of minutes I could hear them all outside, yelling at me, "Charley, hey, come on out. We want to talk to you." But I wouldn't go.

Then I stayed away from the gang for a while. I'd see the fellows in school since we were in the same classes, but I didn't go to the clubhouse, nor join them at the café like I always had. There was no real reason except that I thought I'd try being an individual for a change, instead of just one of a group who all did and thought the same things. And that was mostly what Pat Dalloway said to do and think.

I took to visiting old George as often as I had time for it. He had started a new carving of Knute Rockne which was going to be really great. He let me come into his place now and sit on the bunch of planks and old rags that was his bed. If I just sat and watched him and didn't ask a lot of nosy questions, he ignored me and went on with his work. I usually brought him some tobacco and whatever I could sneak out of the refrigerator behind my mum's back.

At first I pumped him for information. "Say, George, what have you been doing all your life?"

"My life, boy? I lost it. Laid it down for a little and when I went back looking for it, it was too late. Gone. Just like that." He snapped his fingers.

"Where were you the other day?"

"Well, occasionally even an old hermit's got to go down into the morass of humanity." He stepped back viewing his work. "If you can find me another picture of Knute here, why, I'd be very grateful."

"Sure." I knew where there was one. In my dad's picture album. He'd played football when he was at college and was still crazy about the game.

"You ever going to let people see all this some day?" I asked. "When you're ready, I mean?"

"Maybe I should have done drawings with burnt sticks

and red ochre. Of ancient bison and vanished deer. That would have confused a few experts, I'll bet," he answered, almost to himself.

"You know, Charley boy," George seemed to be talking to Knute, but I was listening. "I been thinking. That's a big cave in behind there. You ever have a hankering to do a little carving?"

I shook my head "no", but his back was turned and he didn't see me.

"Old, old," he was muttering to Knute. "Seventy-five, and that's the full allotment. Might not even get to finish this one." He jabbed at Knute's jaw. "It's a way of life, Charley my boy. The only way; creating things. Let others build the cars and roads and houses. You know how long the cave drawings, the ones in southern France, have been around?" He whirled on me with a fierce light in his eye.

I shook my head again.

"Fifteen, maybe twenty thousand years." He glared at me. "How do you like that for beating Old Mister Time?"

I got up to go. It was getting late and I didn't have anything to say to him.

"See you, George."

"Yeh," he grunted.

I didn't go back for three weeks when finally school was over and I was free for the whole summer. I'd been thinking over the last few weeks that I'd spend most of it with old George. Secretly, I'd begun to think about carving. The old boy had something there. I knew he'd teach me. I thought of that long, beautiful, empty cave. We'd haul in firewood and build a nice warming fire which would give us light to work by. People would come from all around.

My parents would be so surprised they'd be speechless. "Do you mean our boy Charles did this?" they'd say to George, and old George would grin and say, "Yep."

I took a loaf of bread, some salami from the cupboard, a pocketful of tobacco from my dad's stock, and slipped off to the cliffs.

Coming up to George's cave, I slowed to catch my breath. When I looked up there, something was terribly wrong. The boards hiding the mouth of the cave were all knocked out, though you still couldn't see it from the trail unless you knew it was there. I stopped to listen a minute, and then I heard voices. I knew those voices.

I burst into George's living room and the shock of it made me sick to my stomach. The whole cave was a mess, completely torn up. The furniture was broken so that it was nothing now but old driftwood boards. A fire had been built right in the middle of the cave out of the orange boxes. But worse than that, the statues had been destroyed. The delicate ones, the ones that had been carved out almost full, were knocked completely loose and lay on the cave floor as a pile of rubbish. The others had heads and arms missing and could never be fixed. Looey, dirty-faced and stupid, was lounging on what was left of the beautiful horse; St George had been scraped out of his saddle completely. The place was dirty. And George was nowhere around.

"Welcome to our new clubhouse, Charley old boy," Pat Dalloway said.

"Where's George?" My tongue seemed too thick to talk.

"You mean that old tramp?" Pat chuckled. "He cleared out after we wrecked the place."

I stepped forward and kicked aside Knute Rockne's face. My fists were clenched.

"You dirty rats!" I screamed. "You dirty, filthy no-good rats! Who gave you the right?"

"Aw, come on, Charley," big fat Chunky was saying. "That old tramp didn't own this cave. We've got as much right to it. We just chased him out and took over, that's all. You helped. We all went in that airhole and found out it ended here."

And that did it. Inside I was all broken up into little pieces. I knew what the outcome would be before I started, but from where I stood, I leaped at Pat and crashed him to the floor. We fought, slugging each other, biting and gouging, rolling over on top of broken statues. Pat was a pretty dirty fighter. He fought to win; no rules. Once I had him on his back and was choking him, but his hand came up with a fistful of sand right into my eyes. From there on he had it all his way. He finished me off and for good measure gave me a couple extra kicks. No one else interfered. They knew it was between Pat and me.

"Get out," he panted. "You don't belong any more."

Butts and Jim dragged me out and threw me down the hill. My bread and salami had scattered all over. They tossed it after me. "So long, Charley," they said.

When I could move, I picked myself up and hobbled away.

Tomorrow I would have two black eyes.

But it isn't over yet. In fact, it's just started.

I've been lying up in my bedroom for three days now, thinking. My mother brings me hot soup and cries a little when she looks at me. My father wanted to go to the police and prosecute, but I wouldn't tell him anything. This is between me and my old gang.

To do a thing like that . . . to destroy an old man's

dream of immortality . . . to tear up what he called his Passport to Paradise . . . well . . . they're going to pay for it, all right.

Tomorrow I'm getting out of bed. I'm going down to the river flats to join the gang that call themselves the River Rats. I'm going to fight every guy in it till I'm the leader.

Then I'm going to lead them to that cave.

Pat Dalloway . . . you are going to get what's coming to you!

Bill and Ted and Chunky. Jim and Butts and Looey . . . you are in for a big surprise . . . When we descend on you . . . when we get through with you . . . you are going to feel just like those statues . . .

Jean McCord

THE 59th STREET BRIDGE SONG

(Feelin' Groovy)

Slow down,
You move too fast.
You got to make the morning last.
Just kickin' down the cobble stones,
Lookin' for fun and feelin' Groovy.

Hello lamppost,
What-cha knowin'?
I've come to watch your flowers growin'.
Ain't-cha got no rhymes for me?
Doot'in' doo-doo, feelin' Groovy.

Got no deeds to do,
No promises to keep.
I'm dappled and drowsy and ready to sleep.
Let the morningtime drop all its petals on me.
Life, I love you.
All is Groovy.

Paul Simon

On a Bicycle

Under the dawn I wake my two-wheel friend.
Shouting in bed my mother says to me,
"Mind you don't clatter it going downstairs!"
I walk him down he springing step to step:

those tyres he has, if you pat him flat-handed
he'll bounce your hand. I mount with an air
and as light a pair of legs as you'll encounter,
slow into Sunday ride out of the gates,
roll along asphalt, press down on the pedals,
speeding, ring, ring, ring, fearless.

Flinging along my happiness my fever,
incapable of breaking out of it,
overtaking the lorries on the road
taking each of them in a single swoop
flying behind them through cut open space
hanging on them uphill. Yes I know.
It's dangerous. I enjoy it. They hoot
and lean out and yell out,
"We'll give you a hand on the hills;
give you some speed; after that
you tear along on your own."
Careering full tilt, pelting along
in a flurry of jokes. Turn a blind eye
to my crazy career; it's the fashion.
You can't tell me how terribly I ride.
One day I'll learn how to ride.

Yevgeny Yevtushenko

TWO VIPERS

"Two Vipers" is one chapter from the book Other Sandals, *a story that takes place in modern day Israel. Adjusting to a new kind of life is often difficult. For Eytan it caused many conflicts because of his own personal problems. What part did the two vipers play in the conflict?*

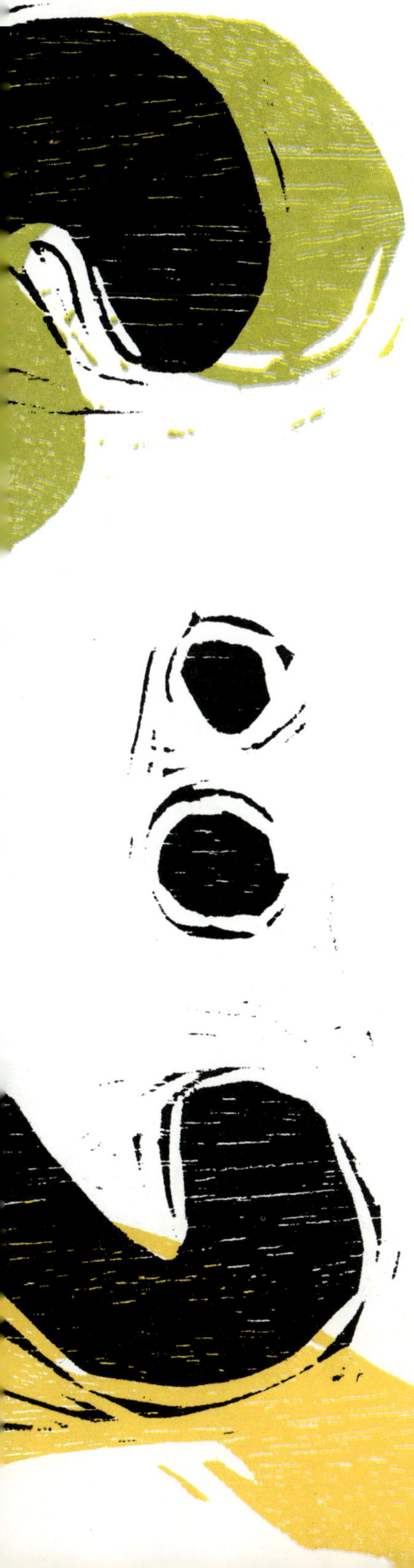

Eytan had come to the kibbutz Kfar Shalom against his will. To be transplanted suddenly from the bustle and excitement of Haifa to the quiet communal farm was difficult enough, but to expose his handicap to other children, to have them stare at his limp, was almost unbearable. Eytan's leg had been badly injured when he was struck by a car the previous summer. Afterwards he refused to help himself, neglecting the exercises that would make his leg strong again. By sending him to Kfar Shalom, his parents hoped that he would become involved again in activities normal to children his age.

Eytan was assigned to Ophir House, where gradually he was forced to assume his share of responsibilities. He began to welcome the friendship of the other children, and soon he was accepted as one of them, a kibbutznik. Only Yael, a girl who was filled with as much bitterness as Eytan, remained aloof and unfriendly.

The time had finally come to work in the orchards. Eytan had resolved to prove his worth to the kibbutz, and turn over a new leaf.

Almost overnight the pears in the orchard had ripened, and everything else at Kfar Shalom took second place in a frenzy of picking before they should get too ripe. All the other jobs on the kibbutz—handicrafts, shoe repairs, carpentry work—were

put aside. Even the library was empty and sewing and mending almost stopped. Children pitched in, according to their ages, and still more hands were needed. Soon truckloads of young people from other kibbutzim arrived to help—and to increase the bad temper of Achim, the overseer.

"He thinks he *owns* the orchards," grumbled one of the boys as they waited in the silvery morning light for the trucks and trailers to take them up to the picking. "Keeps talking about *his* pears!"

Eytam started to answer, but the trucks arrived and there was a rush; and he found himself with Yael and Naomi and a dozen or two of the "imported" pickers, with the rest of Ophir House in another batch altogether.

He looked at Yael gloomily. She didn't look particularly delighted herself. "All we need now," she muttered, "is to get in Achim's section of the orchard!"

They did, of course. He surveyed them all with pessimism as they dragged light aluminium ladders up the rows and adjusted the canvas bags at their waists. He seemed to be just waiting for someone to do something . . .

And it had to be Eytan who did it. He was finding this work a little awkward, anyway, because of his weak leg. It made working on the ladder precarious. He *couldn't* say anything—not with his new leaf and everything—and he didn't know whether to be glad or sorry that no one else had thought of it either.

Within fifteen minutes he was extremely sorry. He never knew exactly how it happened, whether it was the fault of a wobbly leg or a bag not properly fastened, or both; but a dozen ripe pears suddenly cascaded to the ground, and Achim descended on him like Jehovah on Sodom and Gomorrah. "Fool!" he shrieked. "Imbecile! Get out! How dare you ruin my pears!"

All work stopped. From trees on all sides the pickers stared down. Eytan, on the ground with pears in both hands, stared unbelievingly up at the swarthy, black-

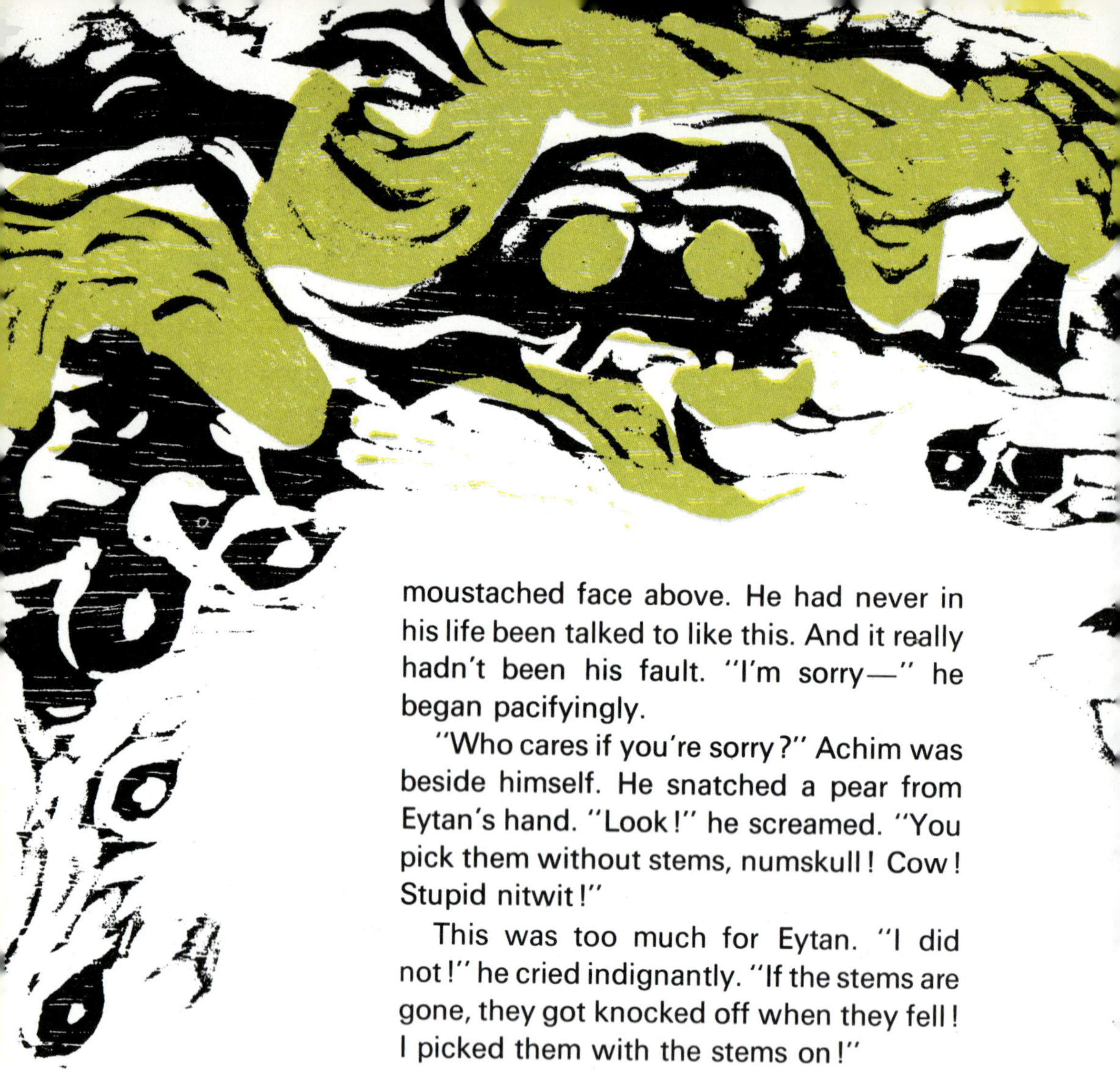

moustached face above. He had never in his life been talked to like this. And it really hadn't been his fault. "I'm sorry—" he began pacifyingly.

"Who cares if you're sorry?" Achim was beside himself. He snatched a pear from Eytan's hand. "Look!" he screamed. "You pick them without stems, numskull! Cow! Stupid nitwit!"

This was too much for Eytan. "I did not!" he cried indignantly. "If the stems are gone, they got knocked off when they fell! I picked them with the stems on!"

Achim paid no attention whatsoever. "You picked them without stems, donkey! Get out of my orchard! Go on!"

Eytan rose to his feet incredulously. Apparently Achim meant it! He was driving him out, dismissing him like a stupid hired hand, and in front of an orchard full of strangers, staring silently from the ladders all around, probably believing that

Eytan *had* picked them without stems! It was ridiculous—nightmarish—and no one spoke up, not even Naomi, who probably hadn't the nerve, or Yael, who probably didn't care or positively rejoiced . . .

His stomach was churning with helpless humiliation. He tried to gather some shreds of dignity around him. After all, he *was* a volunteer and not a paid worker. "I was only trying to help out," he said in a low voice, feeling more of a fool than ever in the continuing silence from the other pickers.

"I don't care! I don't care! You won't ruin any more of my pears! Get out!" And then as Eytan walked stiffly past him, towards the road, Achim sent one more parting shot after him. "Stupid cripple!" he bawled.

Eytan stumbled on blindly, his head high and his face perfectly blank with the effort to keep the hurt from showing. His limp felt six times as noticeable, and the heavy silence continued behind him as he headed back down the row.

It was a long walk back. He trudged along, dazed with hurt and anger, hot tears beginning to prickle behind his eyelids. He blinked them back furiously. He *wasn't* going to let it matter, he told himself untruthfully. He wished he had never come to this beastly place! And it *hadn't* been carelessness, and he *hadn't* picked the pears without stems! That rankled almost as much as the final taunt about cripple.

The narrow road twisted ahead. He'd never walked this way before; he hoped it was the right way back. No, come to think of it, he hoped it wasn't. He didn't want to go back. He didn't want to face anyone. If only he could just get on a bus or something and go home . . .

"Well, the least you can do is let a person catch up!" snapped an extremely cross voice from behind, accompanied by a soft patter of thong sandals in the dust.

Eytan turned just as Yael caught up and fell into step beside him, scowling. "I thought you were supposed to have a bad leg," she told him nastily. "I never saw *anybody* walk so fast!"

Eytan scowled back. "Why aren't you back picking pears with dear Achim?" he demanded, equally nasty.

"Don't be any more stupid than you can help!" Yael glared and kicked the dust deliberately for a few steps with her almost bare feet. "Naomi's gone to tell my father," she added, almost reluctantly. "*He's* Head of Agriculture; *he* can tell that horrid man off! You should have heard him when Naomi and I just climbed down and took off our bags and walked out on him!" She looked pleased for the first time. "I don't expect any of *us* will work for him any more, and he'll have nobody at all once the outsiders are gone. Perhaps we can even get him to leave the kibbutz!"

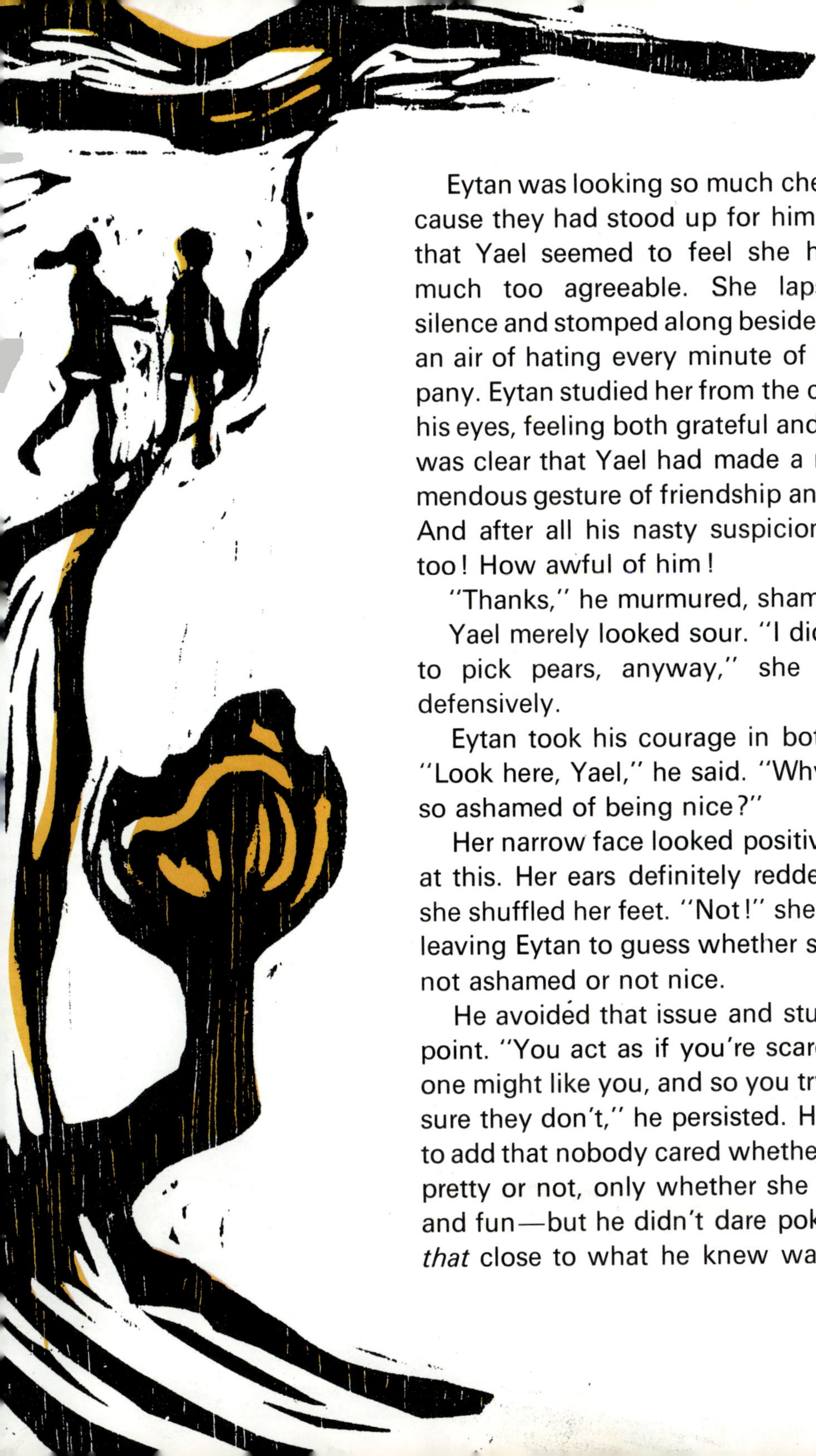

Eytan was looking so much cheered because they had stood up for him after all, that Yael seemed to feel she had been much too agreeable. She lapsed into silence and stomped along beside him with an air of hating every minute of his company. Eytan studied her from the corners of his eyes, feeling both grateful and guilty. It was clear that Yael had made a most tremendous gesture of friendship and loyalty. And after all his nasty suspicions of her too! How awful of him!

"Thanks," he murmured, shamefaced.

Yael merely looked sour. "I didn't want to pick pears, anyway," she muttered defensively.

Eytan took his courage in both hands. "Look here, Yael," he said. "Why are you so ashamed of being nice?"

Her narrow face looked positively bleak at this. Her ears definitely reddened, and she shuffled her feet. "Not!" she growled, leaving Eytan to guess whether she meant not ashamed or not nice.

He avoided that issue and stuck to the point. "You act as if you're scared someone might like you, and so you try to make sure they don't," he persisted. He wanted to add that nobody cared whether she was pretty or not, only whether she was nice and fun—but he didn't dare poke around *that* close to what he knew was her exposed nerve. Instead, he made his voice light and casual. "I mean, why hide your niceness under a barrel?" he went on. "Why not just be yourself and give people a chance to like you?"

And then—for just an instant—he had a glimmering of the truth. That was precisely what Yael was afraid to do! Suppose she gave people a chance to like her for her own nicest self—and they *didn't?* It would be quite unbearable, and she didn't dare risk it. Much safer to be disagreeable to begin with . . .

The glimmering began to get muddled in Eytan's mind, but he had grasped the main point. And he realized too late that he'd hit the nerve after all! Or at least one of them. Yael turned on him furiously.

"Why don't you mind your own business!" she blazed. "I don't want you to like me! Can't you get that through your silly head? You can just go home by yourself; I never wanted to come with you, anyway!"

And she stalked off the road and headed across a stubbly field of harvested grain.

Eytan was no saint. His compassion for Yael was at once submerged in a swift wave of anger. "So who wants you, either!" he yelled. "So go stick your head in a hole and cover it up! So drop dead!"

And as if in instant obedience, Yael stopped short, twisted in an odd leap

backwards, staggered a step and sank to one knee. The face she turned to Eytan was terrified. "Help me!" she quavered. "It bit me!"

Eytan stood for one instant, more horrified even than Yael. It was a snake; he knew it instantly. A viper had got her! He stood still, fighting the need to turn and run beyond even the thought of the loathsome thing. Really, it was too much! He'd already faced self-contempt and got through it; why should he now be confronted with the most awful physical challenge there could possibly be for him? No, he couldn't face it; he really couldn't! Besides, the obviously sensible thing to do was to hurry for help at once. It would be stupid to go out there and risk getting bitten himself, and then there'd be no one at all to help . . .

He found himself off the road, stopping to search frantically for a large stick—a stone—anything! And then, armed with a dead branch in one hand and a rock in the

other, he ran on to Yael, the taste of fear like acid in his mouth.

"Look out," she panted as he ran up. "It was right over there—don't *you* get bitten!" She raised her head to point to a patch of old straw and new-grown weed, then bent it again. She had her small jack-knife out, and—very pale indeed—was setting about the nasty job of slashing deep cuts into the calf of her leg, where four ugly red punctures were oozing blood. Her hand shook a little. "I hate my own blood!" she whispered, her lips nearly white. "I don't mind other people's, but I can't stand my own!"

Eytan was just the opposite. But having steeled himself to come within a scant few metres of a viper, he found this additional challenge quite possible—particularly since it was more urgent than finding the snake. Anyway, it was hardly likely to attack again unless provoked . . . or at least he passionately hoped not.

"Give it here!" he ordered harshly, snatching the knife from Yael and kneeling beside her. She obeyed with unnatural meekness, her face now whiter than ever and covered with sweat. Eytan set his teeth, swallowed hard, prayed that he wouldn't vomit on the spot and cut, quick and hard, into Yael's firm brown leg.

It was hideous! Hideous to feel the knife

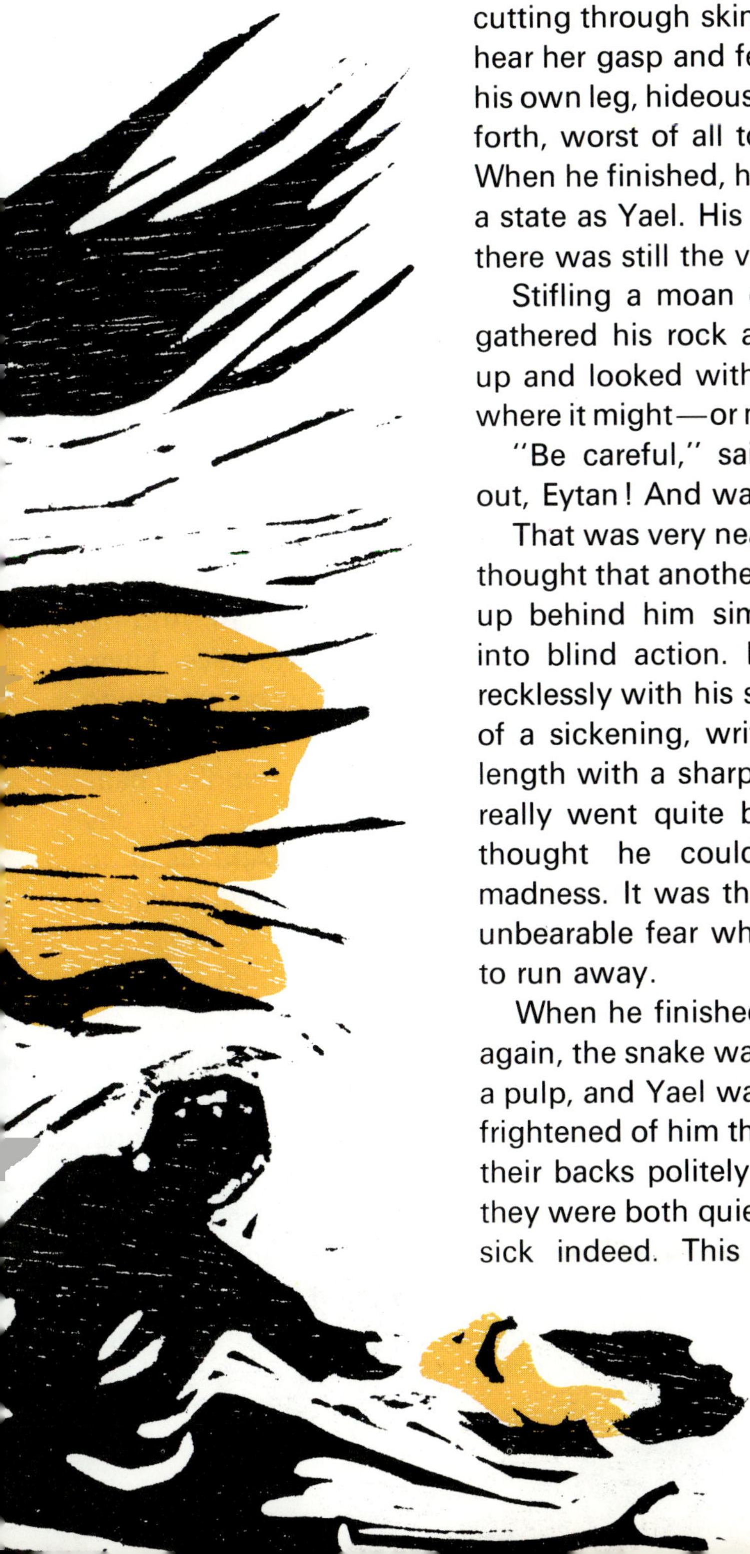

cutting through skin and flesh, hideous to hear her gasp and feel her fingers dig into his own leg, hideous to see the blood gush forth, worst of all to have to do it again! When he finished, he was in nearly as bad a state as Yael. His stomach heaved. And there was still the viper to find and kill.

Stifling a moan of utter refusal, Eytan gathered his rock and stick again, stood up and looked with revulsion at the spot where it might—or might not—be lurking.

"Be careful," said Yael faintly. "Look out, Eytan! And watch for its mate!"

That was very nearly the last straw! The thought that another one might be gliding up behind him simply galvanized Eytan into blind action. He poked the stubble recklessly with his stick, caught a glimpse of a sickening, writhing metre of muddy length with a sharply triangular head and really went quite berserk. Afterwards he thought he could understand battle-madness. It was the outlet you found for unbearable fear when you mustn't use it to run away.

When he finished and came to himself again, the snake was lying there bashed to a pulp, and Yael was looking almost more frightened of him than of the snake. Then, their backs politely turned to each other, they were both quietly and efficiently very sick indeed. This was something they

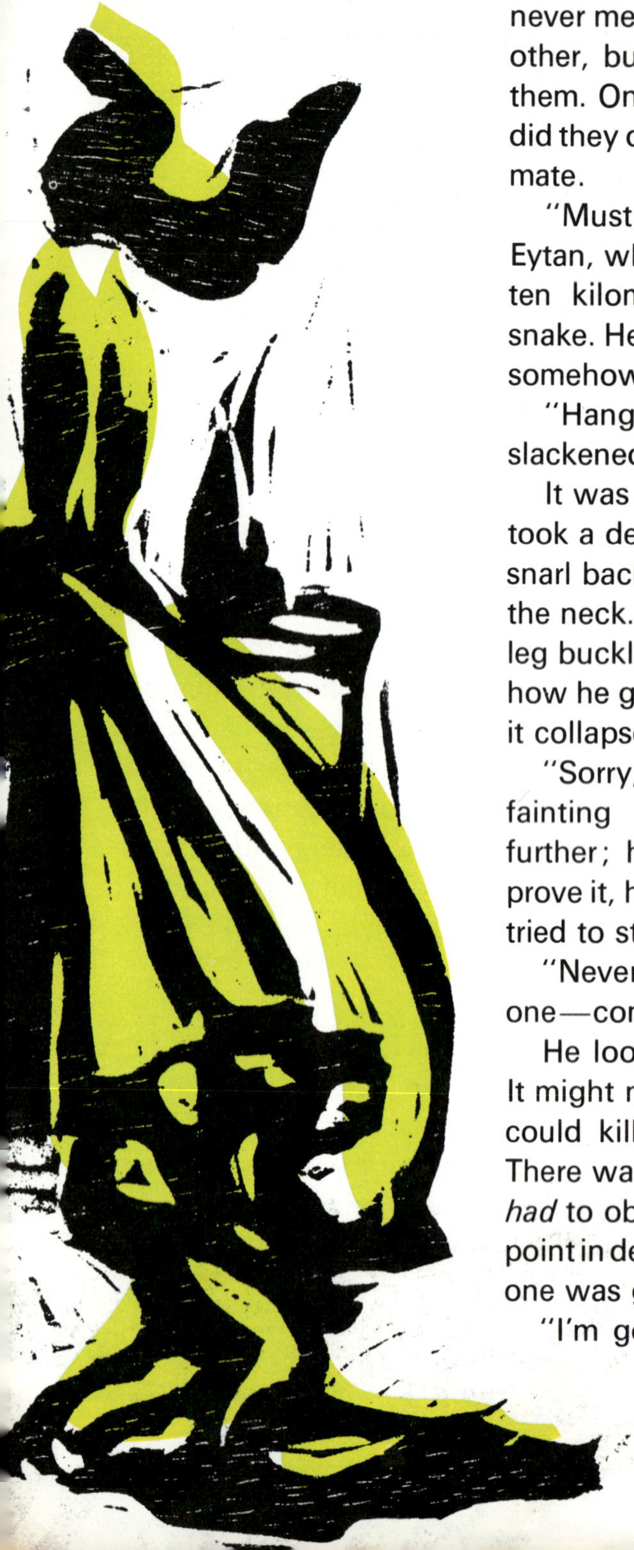

never mentioned afterwards, even to each other, but it was rather a bond between them. Only when they had quite finished, did they once again remember the possible mate.

"Must get you out of here," gulped Eytan, who would rather have carried her ten kilometres than cope with another snake. He somehow got her onto his back, somehow staggered to his feet.

"Hang on!" he snarled as her grip slackened. "Hang on or I'll slap your face!"

It was a silly threat, but it worked. Yael took a deep breath, found the strength to snarl back feebly and gripped him around the neck. It nearly strangled him. And his leg buckled at every step. He never knew how he got back to the road before letting it collapse under the unfair burden.

"Sorry," he gasped to the huddled, half-fainting Yael. "I can't carry you any further; honestly I can't!" And as if to prove it, his leg doubled up again when he tried to stand up.

"Never mind," Yael mumbled. "Some-one—come by—soon."

He looked at her with increasing fear. It might not be soon enough! Viper bites could kill, and Yael was in bad shape. There was simply no choice at all; his leg *had* to obey his will . . . But there was no point in demanding major miracles. A minor one was going to be hard enough.

"I'm going to get help," he told Yael.

"I can't carry you, but I can get help."

There was no reply. Either Yael didn't think it worth a comment, or she was past hearing or speaking or caring. Eytan forced himself to his feet and stood for an instant, thinking. The orchards were possibly a trifle nearer, but Imma Malkah, the kibbutz nurse, and the snake-bite serum were at the main part of the kibbutz. He set out.

It was a nightmarish trip. His leg didn't hurt much; but it kept threatening to quit altogether, so that every step was a major effort. Eytan found himself talking to it,

commanding it to get him there, praying to God to give him the strength he needed.

He passed the barn and the chicken houses, apparently deserted. He passed the neglected craft shack and shoe shop, the carpentry shop and machine shop, the general shower rooms, the cinema grove . . . Wasn't there anyone left on the kibbutz? Ordinarily he'd have seen a dozen people before now!

His leg collapsed once more. Once more he dragged himself up again. "Help!" he shouted with what breath he had. "Help, someone! Please! Help!" And he lurched on towards the infirmary, trying to think what he would do if that, too, were deserted. "Help!"

Ayin House, the first of the living units, was just ahead; and at this last shout, a tiny figure popped out, looking startled. It

was Miryam, Yael's sister. "What's the matter?" she enquired, staring with great interest at Eytan's dusty and blood-spattered condition. "Did you hurt yourself?"

"Miryam!" he gasped. "Get Imma Malkah! Run and get Imma Malkah, quickly!" And then as Miryam still paused, he added the magic word. "Yael needs her, Miryam! Tell Imma Malkah snake bite!" he shouted after the already flying figure which at once shot off towards the infirmary yelling at the top of its voice.

Miryam had a piercing voice, and emergency yells have a special quality. People began to appear from all directions, staring after Miryam and hurrying to Eytan, who was very nearly at the end of his tether.

"Yael—viper—road to pear orchard," he managed as his left leg finally quit and deposited him slowly but definitely on the path. "Yael—viper bit her—road to orchard," he repeated stupidly when Imma Malkah appeared, calm and efficient and armed with snake-bite serum.

"Right," she said, and in a twinkling she had commandeered one of the small cars used to pick up laundry, appointed Chava to come along and help, ordered someone else to phone to Kfar Blum for the doctor and was off in a businesslike cloud of dust.

Eytan, still sitting in the path, stared regretfully after them. He wished he could have gone along, to see it through and to reassure himself about Yael as soon as possible. What if it were too late? But he would only have been a bother now. He had played his part. He sighed and turned his attention back to the growing circle of people around him, all demanding to know exactly what had happened.

He told them, feeling suddenly quite drained and numb. Then he permitted himself to be helped to the infirmary where he parked himself doggedly. He was there watching anxiously, when Imma Malkah brought Yael back. He was there when the doctor arrived. And he was still there when Imma Malkah came out at last and smiled at him and at Imma Mia and Abba Dan, Yael's parents, who had just arrived from the orchards.

"She'll be all right," said Imma Malkah. "Might not have been, but for this boy," she added and fixed a professional eye on Eytan. "Are you all right? That was quite a run, you know; especially for someone with a weak leg!" She looked at him with respect. Yael's parents turned to him. Eytan began to feel embarrassed.

"And now," suggested Imma Malkah presently, "if Dan will just stop trying to pump your arm off at the shoulder and Mia will mop her eyes, I'd suggest something to eat for all of you."

Much, much later Eytan remembered, dimly, as a matter of no importance, that a viper named Achim had publicly humiliated him that morning.

Sally Watson

Boy into Heron

High on a stilt-raised bed above the reeds
He lay and watched the birds, saw the grey heron come,
Perched like himself on long stiff legs,
To search the mud wet shore for frogs and fish,
Marked his grey plumage and the deep slate tail,
And the dark coronet of glossy plumes,
And watching so intently, lost himself,
His own identity merged in the bird's.
And when the heron rose above the lough,
His long legs arrowed in the wind,
His plumes laid flat, the boy took wings,
And rose with him and skimmed across the lake,
And knew the majesty and joy of flight.
Not till the heron grew a distant speck
Beyond his sight, did he, reluctant creep
Into his body's wingless form again.

Celia Randall

This starts out as a story about an ordinary boy who went fishing one ordinary night. Then all of a sudden "the sea exploded in his face" and it became much more than just an ordinary evening.

The Sea Devil

The boy came out of the house and stood quite still, listening. Behind him the lights glowed in the cheerful room, the books were neat and orderly on their shelves, the radio talked importantly to itself. In front of him the bay stretched dark and silent, one of the countless lagoons that border the coast where Florida thrusts its great green thumb deep into the tropics.

It was late September. The night was breathless, with summer's dead hand lying heavy on the land. The tide was beginning to ebb. Somewhere out in the blackness a mullet jumped and fell back with a sullen splash.

The boy turned abruptly and went into the garage where his cast net hung. He was in his late teens, wide-shouldered and strong. He did not have to fish for a living, or even for food; but he liked to go casting alone at night.

He liked the loneliness and the labour of it. He liked the clean taste of salt when he gripped the edge of the net with his teeth, as a net caster must. He liked the arching flight of lead and linen against the starlight, the weltering crash of the net into unsuspecting water. He liked the harsh tug of the retrieving rope around his wrist, and the way the net came alive when the cast was true, and the thud of cap-

tured fish on the floorboards of the skiff.

The boy lifted the net down carefully and lowered it into a bucket. He put a paddle beside the bucket. Then he went into the house. When he came out, he was wearing swimming trunks and a pair of old tennis shoes.

The flat-bottomed skiff was moored off the seawall. He would not go far, he told himself. Just to the tumbledown dock half a kilometre away. Mullet had a way of feeding around old pilings after dark. If he moved quietly, he might pick up two or three in one cast close to the dock. And maybe a couple of others on the way down or back.

He shoved off and stood motionless for a moment, letting his eyes grow accustomed to the dark. Somewhere out in the channel a porpoise blew with a sound like steam escaping. The boy smiled a little; porpoises were his friends. Once, fishing in the Gulf, he had seen the charter boat captain reach overside and gaff a baby porpoise through the sinewy part of the tail. The captain hoisted it aboard and dropped it into the bait-well, where it thrashed around, puzzled and unhappy. And the mother had swum alongside the boat and under the boat and around the boat, nudging the stout planking with her back, slapping it with her tail. The boy had felt sorry for her and made the captain let the baby porpoise go.

He took the net from the bucket, slipped the noose in the retrieving rope over his wrist and pulled the slipknot tight. It was an old net, but still serviceable. He had rewoven the rents made by underwater snags. Then he coiled the nine-metre rope, making sure it had no kinks. A tangled rope, he knew, would spoil any cast.

The basic design of the net, unchanged in three thousand years, was a mesh circle, measuring close to fourteen metres in circumference and could, if thrown perfectly, blanket forty-five square metres of sea water. In the

centre of this radial trap was a small iron collar where the retrieving rope met the twenty-three separate drawstrings leading to the outer rim. Along this rim, spaced three centimetres apart, were the lead sinkers.

The boy raised the iron collar above his head. The net hung soft and pliant and deadly. He shook it gently, making sure that the drawstrings were not tangled and that the sinkers were hanging true. Then he eased it down and picked up the paddle.

The night was as black as a witch's cat, the stars fuzzy and dim. To the south the lights of a causeway made a yellow necklace across the sky. To his left were the tangled roots of a mangrove swamp, and to his right the open waters of the bay. Most of it was fairly shallow, but there were channels two and a half metres deep. The boy could not see the old dock but he knew where it was.

For five minutes he paddled. Then, six metres ahead of the skiff, a mullet jumped. For a moment it hung in the still air, gleaming dully. Then it vanished. Ripples marked the spot, and where there was one there were often others.

The boy stood up quickly. He picked up the coiled rope and with the same hand grasped the net at a point a metre below the iron collar. Raising the skirt to his mouth, he gripped it strongly with his teeth and slid his free hand as far as it would go down the circumference of the net. He waited with feet planted solidly experiencing the fierce exhilaration of the hunter at the moment of ambush.

A mullet swirled ahead and to the left. The boy swung the heavy net back and shot it forward, letting go simultaneously with his rope hand and his teeth. With the other hand he held on a fraction of a second longer to give the spin that would flare his net into a circle. The skiff ducked sideways, but the boy kept his balance. The net fell with a splash.

In five seconds he began to retrieve it, pulling with a series of sharp jerks so that the drawstrings would gather the net inward. It was like a giant fish closing on this segment of the teeming sea. The net quivered, and he knew it was not empty. He swung it, dripping, over the gunwale and saw the broad silver side of the mullet quivering, saw too the gleam of a smaller fish. He looked closely to make sure no stingray was hidden in the mesh, then raised the iron collar and shook the net out.

The mullet fell with a thud and flapped wildly. The other victim was an angel fish, beautifully marked but too small to keep. The boy picked it up gently and dropped it overboard. He coiled the rope and took up the paddle. He would cast no more until he came to the dock.

The skiff moved on. At last, three metres apart, a pair of stakes rose up gauntly out of the night. Barnacle encrusted, they had once marked the approach from the main channel. The boy guided the skiff between them and put the paddle down softly. He stood up, reached for the net and tightened the noose around his wrist. From here he could drift down upon the dock. He could see it now, a ruined skeleton in the starshine. Beyond it a mullet jumped and fell back with a flat, liquid sound. The boy raised the edge of the net and put it between his teeth. He would not cast at a single swirl, he decided, only at two or three together. The skiff was barely moving. He felt his muscles tense themselves, awaiting the signal from the brain.

Behind him in the channel he heard the porpoise blow again, nearer now. He frowned in the darkness. If the porpoise chose to fish here, the mullet would scatter and vanish. There was no time to lose.

A school of sardines surfaced suddenly, skittering along like drops of mercury. Something, perhaps the shadow of the skiff, had frightened them. The old dock loomed very close. A mullet broke water just too far away; then another, nearer. The boy decided to wait no longer.

He swung back the net, heavier now that it was wet. He had to turn his head, but out of the corner of his eye he saw two swirls in the black water, just off the starboard bow. They were about two and a half metres apart, and they had the sluggish oily look that marks the presence of something big just below the surface. His conscious mind had no time to function, but instinct told him that the net was wide enough to cover both swirls if he altered the direction of his cast. He could not halt the swing, but he shifted his

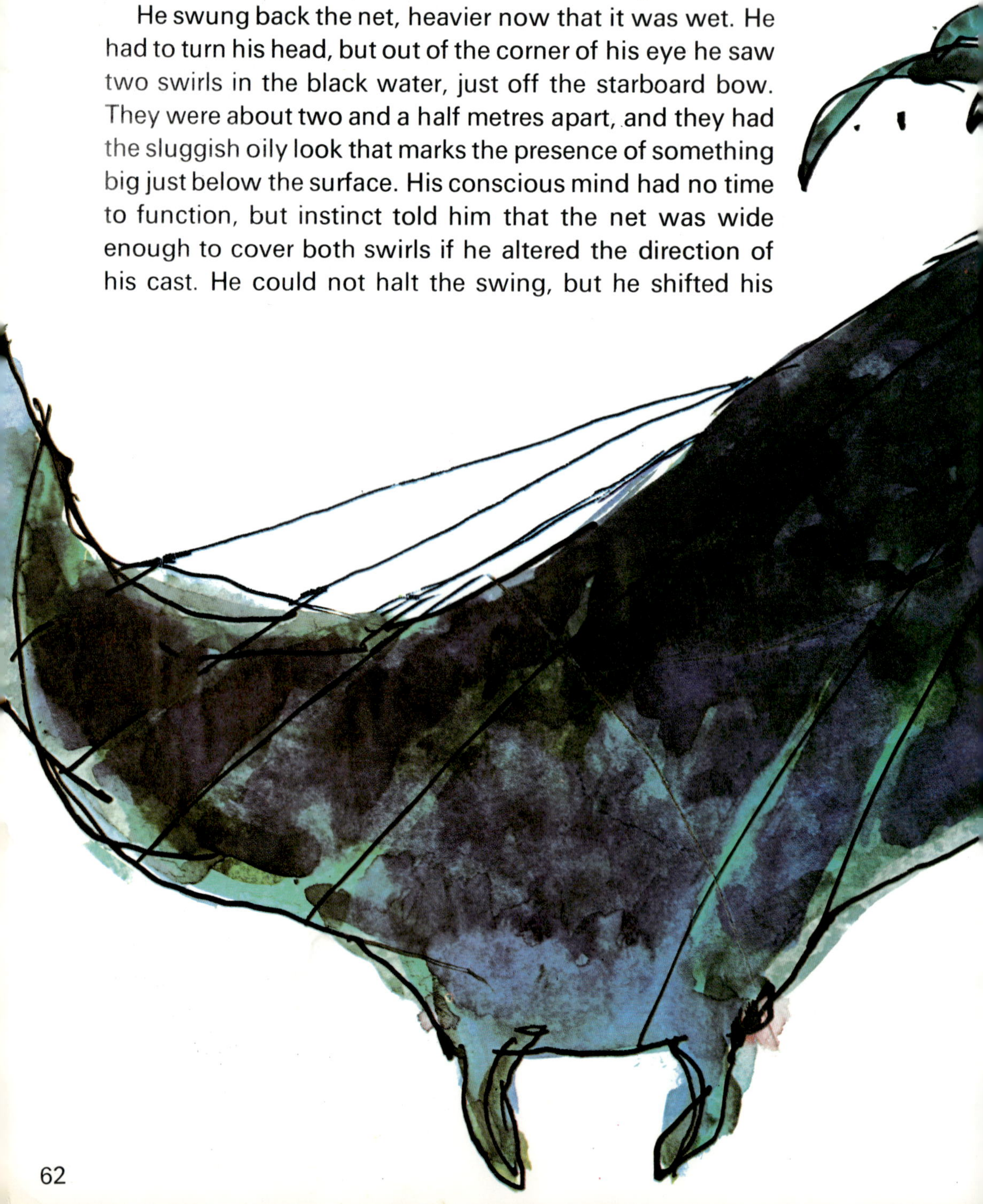

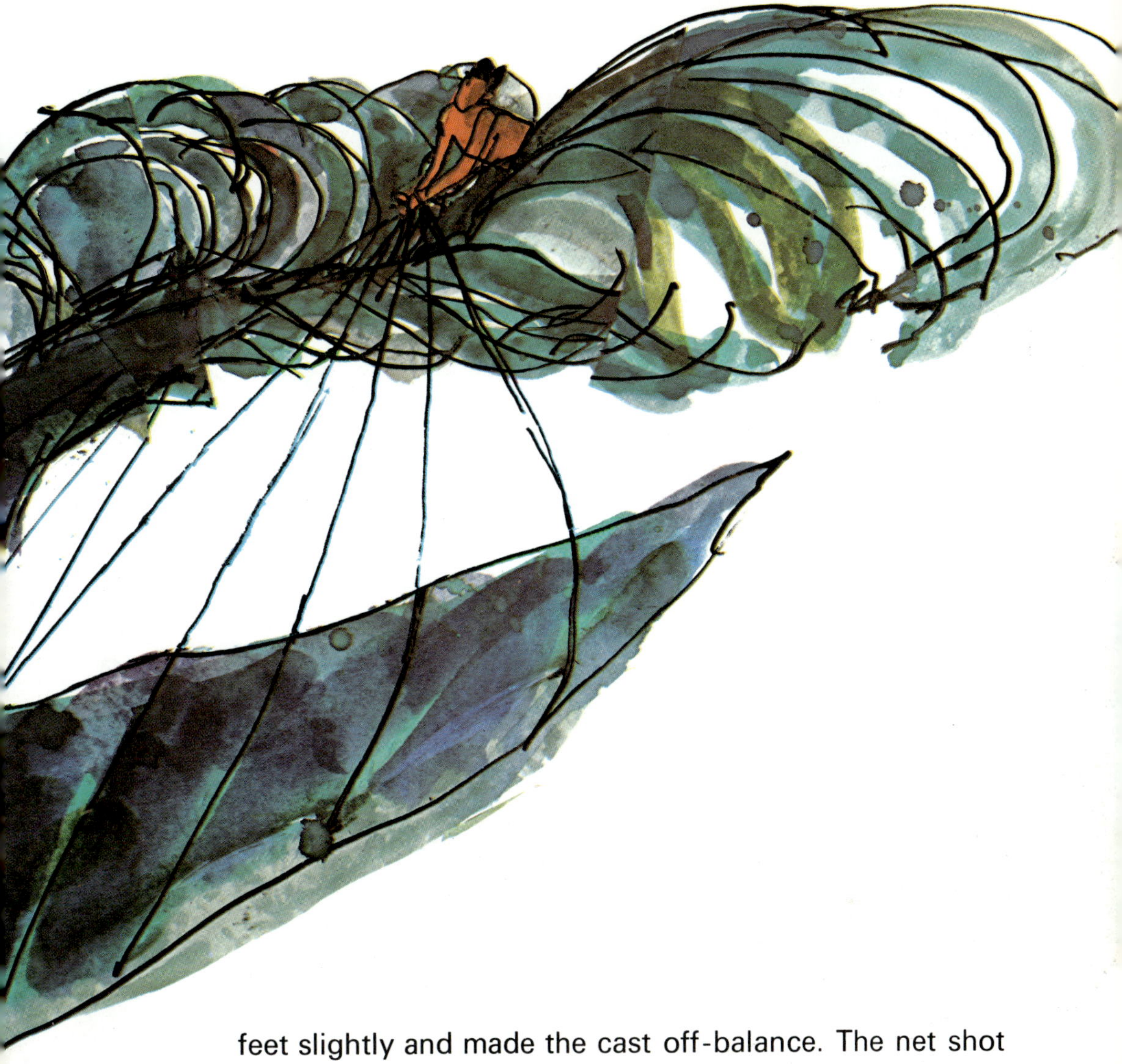

feet slightly and made the cast off-balance. The net shot forward, flared into an oval and dropped just where he wanted it to.

Then the sea exploded in his face. In a frenzy of spray, a great horned thing shot like a huge bat out of the water. The boy saw the mesh of his net etched against the mottled blackness of its body; and he knew in the split second that those twin swirls had been made not by two mullet, but by the wing tips of a giant ray. It was a *Manta birostris*, also

known as a clam cracker, devil ray or sea devil.

The boy gave a hoarse cry, trying to claw the slipknot off his wrist; but there was no time. The thin line snapped taut. He shot over the side of the skiff as if he had roped a runaway locomotive. Hitting the water headfirst, he bounced once and then ploughed a blinding furrow for perhaps ten metres. Then the line went slack as the sea devil jumped again. Although not full grown, it was close to three metres from tip to tip and weighed over four hundred and fifty kilograms. Up into the air it went, its pearl-coloured underbelly gleaming as it twisted in a frantic effort to dislodge the clinging thing that had fallen upon it. Up into the starlight, a monstrous survival from the dawn of time.

The water was less than a metre deep. Sobbing and choking, the boy struggled for a foothold on the slimy bottom. Sucking in great gulps of air, he fought to free himself from the rope. But the slipknot was jammed deep into his wrist. He might as well have tried to loosen a circle of steel.

The ray came down with a thunderous splash and drove

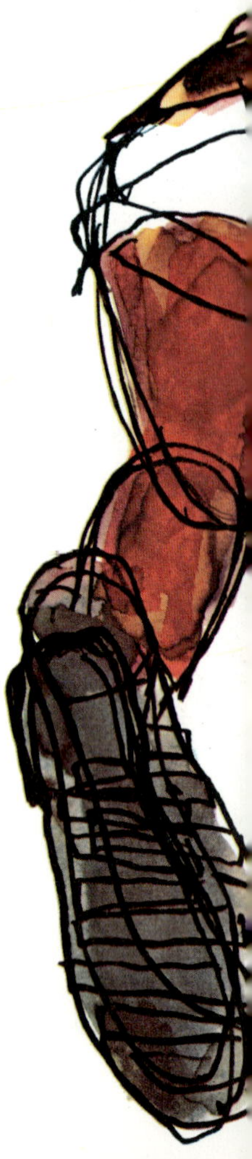

forward again. The flexible net followed every movement, impeding it hardly at all. The boy braced for the shock with desperate strength, but the effort was useless. His arm straightened out with a jerk that seemed to dislocate his shoulder; his feet shot out from under him; his head went under again. Now at last he knew how a fish must feel when the line tightens and drags him towards the alien element that is his doom. Now he knew.

Desperately he dug the fingers of his free hand into the ooze and felt them dredge a futile channel through broken shells and ribbonlike sea grasses. He tried to raise his head but could not get it clear. Torrents of spray choked him as the ray plunged towards deep water.

His eyes were of no use in the foam-streaked blackness. He closed them tight, and an insane sequence of pictures flashed through his mind. He saw his family sitting in their living room, waiting calmly for his return. He saw the mullet he had just caught gasping its life away on the floor-boards of the skiff. He saw these and other things as his body fought silently and tenaciously for life. His hand touched something hard and closed on it in a death grip, but it was only the sharp-edged helmet of a horseshoe crab. After an instant he let it go.

He had been underwater for perhaps fifteen seconds now, and something in his brain told him quite calmly that he could last another half minute. Then the red flashes behind his eyes would merge into darkness, and water would pour into his lungs in one painful shock, and he would be finished.

This thought spurred him to a desperate effort. He reached up and caught his pinioned wrist with his free hand. He doubled up his knees to create more drag. He thrashed his body madly, like a fighting fish, from side to side. This did not disturb the ray; but now one of the great wings tore through the mesh, the net slipped lower over the fins projecting like horns from below the nightmare

head and the sea devil jumped again.

Once more the boy was able to get his feet on the bottom and his head above water, and he saw ahead of him the pair of ancient stakes that marked the approach to the channel. He knew that if he was dragged much beyond those stakes he would be in two and a half metres of water. Then the ray would go down to hug the bottom as rays always do, and no power on earth could save him. In this moment of pause he flung himself towards the stakes.

For a moment he thought that his captor yielded a bit. Then the ray moved off again, but more slowly now, and for a few metres the boy was able to keep his feet on the bottom. Twice he hurled himself back against the rope with all his strength, hoping that something would break, but nothing did. The mesh of the net was ripped and torn, but the draw lines were strong.

The boy now had no feeling in his trapped hand. The ray, feeling the powerful lunges of an unknown thing trying to restrain it, drove its great wings against the unyielding water. It forged ahead, dragging the boy and pushing a sullen wave in front of it.

The boy had swung as far as he could towards the stakes. He plunged towards one and missed it by a hair's breadth. His feet slipped and he went down on his knees. The ray swerved sharply, and the second stake came right at him. He reached out with his free hand and caught it.

The razor-sharp barnacles bit into his hand, collapsed under the pressure and drove tiny, slime-covered shell splinters deep into his flesh. He felt the pain and welcomed it, and he made his fingers into an iron claw that would hold until the tendons were severed or the skin was shredded from the bone. The ray felt a jerk that stopped it dead in the water. For a moment all was still.

Then the net slipped again, blinding the sea devil's eyes momentarily. It settled to the bottom and, bracing its wings against the mud, hurled itself forward and upwards.

The stake was only small, and it was old. Ten thousand tides had swirled around it. Worms had bored; parasites had clung. Under the crust of barnacles it still had some heart left, but not enough. The boy's grip was one and a half metres above the floor of the bay; the leverage was too great. The stake snapped off at its base.

The ray lunged upwards, dragging the boy and the useless timber. When the stake snapped, the boy had his lungs full of air, and he thought of expelling the air and inhaling water so as to end it all quickly. He thought of this, but he did not do it. And then, just at the channel's edge, the ray met the porpoise coming in towards the dock.

The porpoise had fed well and was in no hurry. It had no quarrel with any ray, but it feared no fish in the sea. When the great black shadow came rushing blindly and unavoidably, the porpoise rolled fast and struck once with its massive horizontal tail.

The blow descended on the ray's flat body with a sound like a pistol shot. It would have broken a buffalo's back, and even the sea devil was half-stunned. Veering wildly, it turned back towards shallow water and passed within three metres of the boy. It slowed and almost stopped, wing tips moving faintly, gathering strength for another rush.

The boy had heard the tremendous slap of the great mammal's tail and the snorting gasp as it plunged away. He felt the line go slack, and raising his dripping face, he reached for the bottom with his feet. He found it, but now the water was up to his neck.

He plucked at the noose once more with his lacerated hand, but there was no strength in his fingers. As the ray began to move again, tension came back into the line. For half a second the boy was tempted to throw himself backwards and fight as he had been doing, pitting his strength against the vastly superior strength of the brute.

But the acceptance of imminent death had done something to his brain. It had driven out the fear, and with fear had gone the panic. He could think now, and he knew that if he was to make any use of this last chance, it would have to be based on reason. Only by using his brain could he possibly survive.

He did not know whether his body still had the strength to carry out the brain's commands, but he began to swim forward towards the ray that was still moving hesitantly away from the channel. He swam forward, feeling the rope go slack as he gained on the creature.

Ahead of him he saw the one remaining stake, and he made himself swim faster until he was parallel with the ray and the rope trailed behind both of them in a deep U. He swam with a surge of desperate energy and was slightly in the lead as they came to the stake. He passed on one side of it; the ray was on the other.

Then the boy took one last deep breath and went down under the black water until he was sitting on the bottom of the bay. He put one foot over the line so that it passed under his bent knee. He drove both heels into the mud and clutched the slimy grass with his bleeding hand, waiting for the tension to come again.

The ray passed on the other side of the stake, moving faster now. The rope grew taut again, and it began to drag the boy back towards the stake. He held his prisoned wrist close to the bottom, under his knee, and he prayed that the stake would not break.

He felt the rope vibrate as the barnacles bit into it. He did not know whether the rope would crush the barnacles, or whether the barnacles would cut the rope. All he knew was that in five seconds or less he would be dragged into the stake and cut to ribbons if he tried to hold on; or drowned if he didn't.

He felt himself sliding slowly, and then faster, and suddenly the ray made a great leap forward. The rope burned

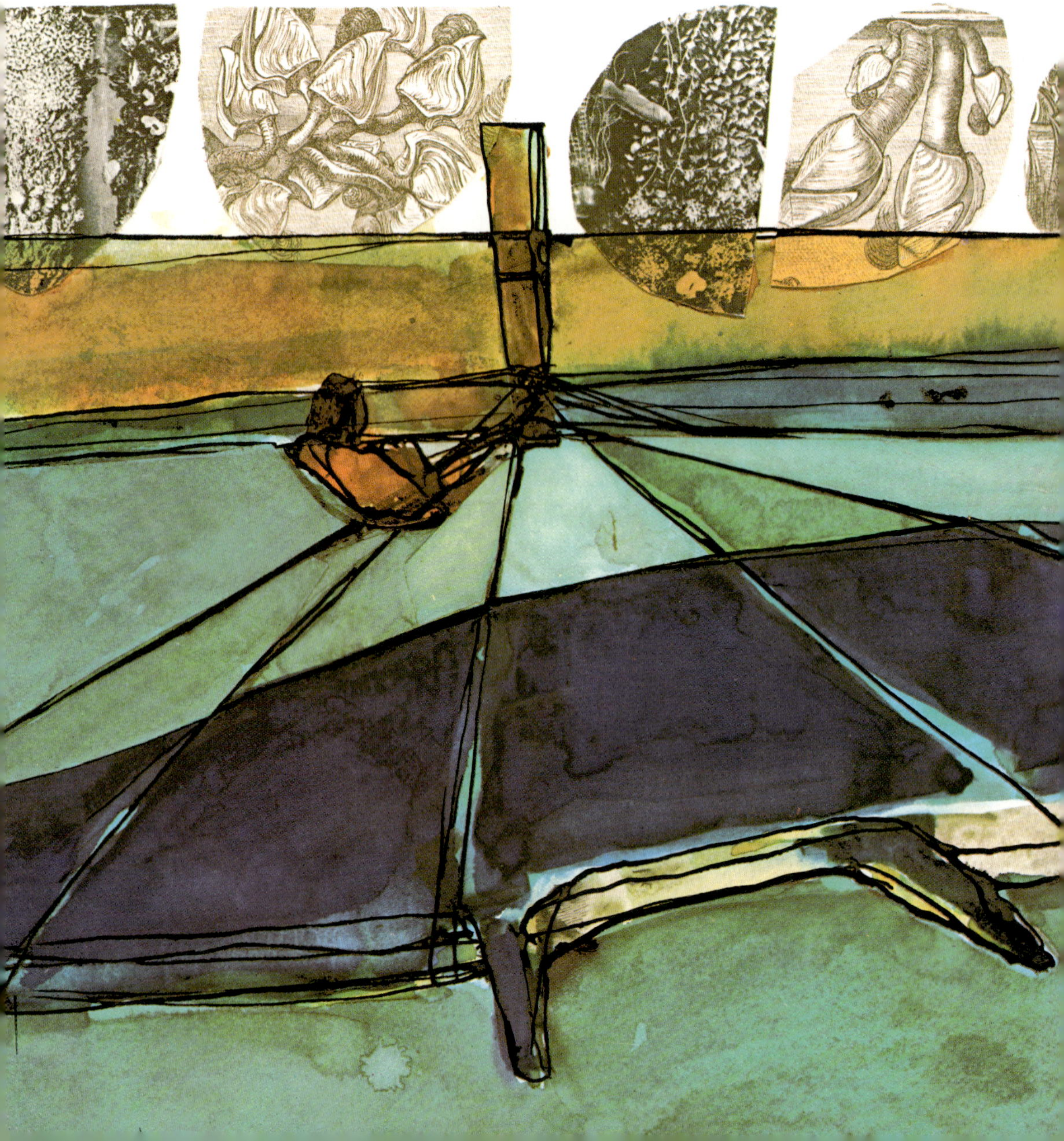

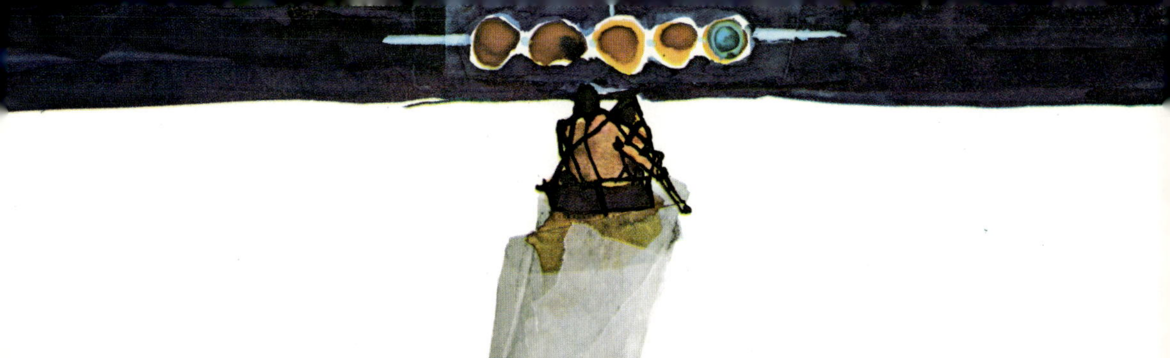

around the base of the stake. Hitting the stake hard with his foot, the boy kicked himself backward with his remaining strength. The rope parted, and he was free.

He came slowly to the surface. Nine metres away the sea devil made one tremendous leap and disappeared into the darkness. The boy raised his wrist and looked at the frayed length of rope dangling from it. Half a metre, perhaps. He lifted his other hand and felt the hot blood start instantly, but he didn't care. He put this hand on the stake above the barnacles and held on to the good rough honest wood. He heard a strange noise and realized that it was himself sobbing.

From high above came a droning sound. Looking up, he saw the night plane from New Orleans inbound for Tampa. Calm and serene it sailed, a symbol of man's proud mastery over nature. Its lights winked red and green for a moment. Then it was gone.

Slowly, painfully, the boy began to move through the placid water. He came to the skiff at last and climbed into it. The mullet, still alive, slapped convulsively with its tail. The boy reached down with his torn hand, picked up the mullet and let it go.

He began to work on the slipknot doggedly with his teeth. His mind was almost a blank, but not quite. He knew one thing. He knew he would do no more casting alone at night. Not in the dark of the moon. No, not he.

Arthur Gordon

Gulls Land and Cease To Be

Spread back across the air, wings wide,
legs out, the wind delicately
dumped in balance, the gulls ride
down, down, land, and exactly
touch, folding not quite at once
into their gangling weight, but
taking one step, two, wings still askance,
reluctantly, at last, shut,
twitch one look around
and are aground.

John Ciardi

Escape from war-torn Curacao was cut short when a torpedo hit the freighter that Phillip was aboard. After drifting on a raft for a few days, Timothy, an ancient black West Indian, and eleven-year-old Phillip, and perhaps even Stew Cat were grateful to find themselves on a tiny Caribbean islet. A blow on the head during the sinking of the freighter left Phillip blind after the second day on the raft. This blindness was only one of the problems that Phillip had to face in living with Timothy and learning to care for himself on this deserted island.

Phillip tells his own story.

ON THE CAY

During those first few days on the island, the times I spent alone were terrible. It was, of course, being unable to see that made all the sounds so frightening. I guess if you are born blind, it is not so bad. You grow up knowing each sound and what it means.

Suddenly, the tears came out. I knew it was not a manly thing to do, something my father would have frowned on, but I couldn't stop. Then from nowhere came Stew Cat. He rubbed along my arms and up against my cheek, purring hard. I held him close.

Soon, Timothy came up the hill, shouting, "Young bahss, tree nice langosta."

I refused to speak to him because he had left me for such a long time.

He stood over me and said, "'Ere, touch dem, dey are still alive." He was almost crowing over his lobster.

I turned away. Sooner or later, Timothy would have to understand that he could not ignore me one minute and then treat me as a friend the next.

He said softly, "Young bahss, be an outrageous mahn if you like, but 'ere I'm all you got."

I didn't answer.

He roasted the langosta over the fire, and later we crawled into the hut to spend our first night on the silent island.

Timothy seemed very tired and groaned a lot. Before we went to sleep, I asked him, "Tell me the truth, Timothy, how old are you?"

He sighed deeply, "More dan seventy. Eben more dan seventy. . ."

He was very old. Old enough to die there.

In the morning, Timothy began making the fire pile down on the beach. He had a plan. We'd always keep a small fire smouldering up by the hut, and if an aeroplane came near, he'd take a piece of burning wood from our small fire to ignite the big one. That way, he said, we could save the few matches that we had.

It didn't take him long to stack driftwood over dried palm fronds. Then he said, "Now, young bahss, we mus' say somethin' on d'san'."

Sometimes it was difficult to understand Timothy. The soft and beautiful West Indian accent and way of speaking weren't always clear.

"Say something on the sand?" I asked.

"So dey be knowin' we are downg 'ere," he explained.

"Who?"

"D'mahn in d'sky, of course."

"Oh." Now I understood.

I guess Timothy was standing there looking at me, waiting for me to say something or do something. I heard him say, "Well, young bahss."

"What do we do now?" I asked.

His voice now impatient, he said, "Say somethin' wid d'rock, wid many rock; eeevery rock be sayin' somethin'. . ."

I frowned at him. "I don't think I can help you, Timothy. I can't see any rocks."

Timothy groaned. "I can see d'rock, young bahss. But what do we say?"

I laughed at him, enjoying it now. "We say 'help'."

He grunted in satisfaction.

For the next twenty or thirty minutes, I could hear Timothy dropping rocks against each other, singing softly to himself in calypso. It was a song about "fungee an' feesh". I'd had "fungi" in Willemstad down in the blacks' market at Ruyterkade. It was just plain corn meal. But most food has different names in the islands.

Soon, he came to stand over me. "Now, young bahss," he said. He seemed to be waiting.

"Yes?"

There was a silence until Timothy broke it with anguish. "Wid d'rock, say 'help'."

I looked up in his direction and suddenly understood that Timothy could not spell. He was just too stubborn, or too proud, to admit it.

I nodded and began feeling around the sand for a stick.

He asked, "What you reachin' for?"

"A stick to make lines with."

He placed one in my hands, and I carefully lettered H-E-L-P on the sand while he stood above me, watching. He kept murmuring, "Ah-huh, ah-huh," as if making sure I was spelling it correctly.

When I had finished, Timothy said approvingly, "I tell you, young bahss, dat do say help." Then he happily arranged the rocks on the sand, following my lines.

I felt good. I knew how to do something that Timothy couldn't do. *He couldn't spell.* I felt superior to Timothy that day, but I let him play his little game, pretending not to know that he really couldn't spell.

In the afternoon, Timothy said we'd make a rope.

On the north end of the island, tough vines, almost as large as a pencil, were laced over the sand. It took us several hours to tear out a big pile of them. Then Timothy began weaving a rope that would stretch all the way down the hill to the beach and fire pile.

The rope was for me. If he happened to be out on the reef and I heard a plane, I could take a light from our campfire, follow the rope down and touch off the big fire. The vine rope would also serve to get me safely down to the beach.

After we'd torn the vines out, and he was weaving the rope, he said, "Young bahss, you mus' begin to help wid d'udder wark."

We were sitting up by the hut. I had my back to a palm and was thinking that back in Willemstad, at this moment,

I'd probably be sitting in a classroom, three desks away from Henrik, listening to Herr Jonckheer talk about European history. I'd been tutored in Dutch the first year in Willemstad so I could attend the local school. Now I could speak it and understand it.

My hands were tired from pulling the vines, and I just wanted to sit and think. I did not want to work. I said, "Timothy, I'm blind. I can't see to work."

I heard him cutting something with his sharp knife. He replied softly, "D'han' is not blin'."

Didn't the old man understand? To work, apart from pulling up vines or drawing something in the sand, you must be able to see.

Stubbornly, he said, "Young bahss, we need sleepin' mats. You can make d'mats."

I looked over in his direction. "You do it," I said.

He sighed back, saying, "D'best matmaker in Charlotte Amalie, downg in Frenchtown, b'total blin'."

"But he's a man, and he has to do that to make a living."

"B'true," Timothy said quietly.

But in a few minutes, he placed several lengths of palm fibre across my lap. He really was an old mule. "D'palm mat is veree easy. Jus' ovah an' under . . ."

Becoming angry with him, I said, "I tell you, I can't see."

He paid no attention to me. "Take dis' han' hol' d'palm like dis; den ovah an' under; den more palm."

I could feel him standing there watching me as I tried to reeve the lengths, but I knew they weren't fitting together. He said, "Like dis, I tell you," and reached down to guide my hand. "Ovah an' under . . ."

I tried again, but it didn't work. I stood up, threw the palm fibres at him and screamed. "I won't do it! You're stupid, you can't even spell . . ."

Timothy's heavy hand struck my face sharply.

Stunned, I touched my face where he'd hit me. Then I turned away from where I thought he was. My cheek stung, but I wouldn't let him see me with tears in my eyes.

I heard him saying very gently, "B'gettin' back to wark, my own self."

I sat down again.

He began to sing that "fungee and feesh" song in a low voice, and I could picture him sitting on the sand in front of the hut; that tangled grey hair, the black face and those great horny hands winding the strands of vine.

The rope, I thought. It wasn't for him. It was for me.

After a while, I said, "Timothy . . ."

He did not answer, but walked over to me, pressing more palm fronds into my hands. He murmured, "'Tis veree easy, ovah an' under . . ." Then he went back to singing about fungee and feesh.

Something happened to me that day on the cay. I'm not quite sure what it was even now, but I had begun to change.

I said to Timothy, "I want to be your friend."

He said softly, "Young bahss, you 'ave always been my friend."

I said, "Can you call me Phillip instead of young boss?"

"Phill-eep," he said warmly.

During our seventh night on the island, it rained. It was one of those tropical storms that comes up swiftly without warning. We were asleep on the palm mats that I'd made, but it awakened us immediately. The rain sounded like bullets hitting on the dried palm-frond roof. We ran out into it, shouting and letting the fresh water hit our bodies. It was cool and felt good.

Timothy yelled that his catchment was working. He had taken more boards from the top of the raft and had made

a large trough that would catch the rain. He'd picked up bamboo lengths on the beach and had fitted them together into a short pipe to funnel the rain water into our keg.

It rained for almost two hours, and Timothy was quite angry with himself for not making a second catchment because the keg was soon full and overflowing.

We stayed out in the cool rain for twenty or thirty minutes and then went back inside. The roof leaked badly but we didn't mind. We got on our mats and opened our mouths to the sweet, fresh water. Stew Cat was huddled in a ball over in a corner, Timothy said, not enjoying it at all.

I liked the rain because it was something I could hear

and feel; not something I must see. It peppered in bursts against the frond roof, and I could hear the drips as it leaked through. The squally wind was in the tops of the palms and I could imagine how they looked in the night sky, thrashing against each other high over our little cay.

I wanted it to rain all night.

We talked for a long time when the rain began to slacken off. Timothy asked me about my mother and father. I told him all about them and about how we lived in Scharloo, getting very lonely and homesick while I was telling him. He kept saying, "Ah, dat be true?"

Then Timothy told me what he could remember from his own childhood. It wasn't at all like mine. He'd never gone to school, and was working on a fishing boat by the time he was ten. It almost seemed that the only fun he had was once a year at carnival when he'd put frangipani leaves round his ankles and dress up in a donkey hide to parade round with *mocki jumbis*, the spirit chasers, while the old ladies of Charlotte Amalie danced the *bambola* around them.

He chuckled. "I drink plenty rhum dose tree days of carnival."

I could picture him in his donkey skin, wheeling around to the music of steel bands. They had them in Willemstad too.

Because it had been on my mind I told him that my mother didn't like black people and asked him why.

He answered slowly, "I don' like some white people my own self, but 'twould be outrageous if I didn' like any o' dem."

Wanting to hear it from Timothy, I asked him why there were different colours of skin, white and black, brown and red, and he laughed back, "Why b'feesh different colour, or flower b'different colour? I true don' know, Phill-eep, but I true tink beneath d'skin is all d'same."

Herr Jonckheer had said something like that in school, but it did not mean quite as much as when Timothy said it.

Long after he'd begun to snore in the dripping hut, I thought about it. Suddenly, I wished my father and mother could see us there together on the little island.

I moved close to Timothy's big body before I went to sleep. I remember smiling in the darkness. He felt neither white nor black.

In the morning, the air was crisp and the cay smelt fresh and clean. Timothy cooked a small fish, a pompano, that

he'd speared at dawn down on the reef. Neither of us had felt so good or so clean since we had been aboard the *Hato*. And without discussing it, we both thought this might be the day an aircraft would swing up into the Devil's Mouth, if that's where we were.

The pompano, broiled over the low fire, tasted good. Of course, we were eating little but what came from the sea. Fish, langosta, mussels or the eggs of sea urchins, those small, black round sea animals with sharp spines that attach themselves to the reefs.

Timothy had tried to make a stew from seaweed, but it tasted bitter. Then he'd tried to boil some new sea-grape roots but they made us ill. The only thing that ever worked for him was sea-grape leaves, boiled first in sea water and then cooked in fresh water.

But above us, twelve metres from the ground, Timothy said, was a feast. Big, fat green coconuts. When we'd landed, there were a few dried ones on the ground, but the meat in them was not very tasty. In a fresher one, there was still some milk, but it was rancid.

At least once a day, especially when we were around the hut, Timothy would say, " 'Tis outrageous dem coconut hang up in d'sky when we could use d'milk an' meat." Or he'd say, "Timothy, my own self, long ago could climb d'palm veree easy." Or hinting, and I guess he was probably looking up at them, "Phill-eep, I do believe you b'gettin' outrageous strong 'ere on d'islan'."

He made a point of saying that if he were only fifty again, he could climb the tree and slice them off with his knife. But at seventy-odd years, he did not think he could make it to the top.

That morning over breakfast, Timothy said, looking to the tops of the palms, I'm sure, "A lil' milk from d'coconut would b'good now, eh, Phill-eep?"

As yet, I didn't have the courage to climb the palms. "Yes, it would," I said.

Timothy cleared his throat, sighed deeply and put the coconuts out of his mind. But I knew he'd try me again.

He said, "Dem devilin' coconuts aside, your mutthur would never be knowin' you now."

I asked why.

"You are veree brown an' veree lean," he said.

I tried to imagine how I looked. I knew my shirt and pants were in tatters. My hair felt ropy. There was no way to comb it. I wondered how my eyes looked and asked Timothy about that.

"Dey look widout cease," he said. "Dey stare, Phill-eep."

"Do they bother you?"

Timothy laughed. "Not me. Eeevery day I tink what rare good luck I 'ave dat you be 'ere wid my own self on dis outrageous, hombug islan'."

I thought awhile and then asked him, "How long was it before that friend of yours, that friend in the Barbados, could see again?"

Timothy replied vaguely, "Oh, many mont', I do recall."

"But you told me on the raft it was only three days."

"Did I say dat?"

"Yes!"

"Well," Timothy said, " 'twas a long time ago. But 'e got 'is sight back, to be true." He paused a moment, then said, "Now, I tell you, we got much wark to do today."

I noticed more and more that Timothy always changed the subject when we began to talk about my eyes. He would make any kind of an excuse.

"What work?" I asked.

"Now, lemme see," he said. "For one ting, we mus' make another catchment . . . an' we mus' go to d'reef for food . . . an' . . ."

I waited.

Timothy finally exploded. "Now, dat is a lot o' wark, Phill-eep, to be true."

Timothy had fashioned a cane for me, and I was now

using it to feel my way around the island. I fell down often, but unless I fell into sea grape, it did not hurt. Even then, I only got a few scratches.

Slowly, I was beginning to know the island. By myself, keeping my feet in the damp sand, which meant I was near the water, I walked the whole way around it. Timothy was very proud of me.

From walking over it, feeling it and listening to it, I think I knew what our cay looked like. As Timothy said, it was shaped like a melon, or a turtle, sloping up from the sea to our ridge where the palms flapped all day and night in the light trade wind.

The beach, I now believed, was about thirty-six metres wide in most places, stretching all the way around the island. On one end, to the east, was a low coral reef that extended several hundred metres, awash in many places.

I know it was to the east because one morning I was down there with Timothy when the sun came up, and I could feel the warmth on my face from that direction.

The sea grape, a metre tall at the edge of the beach, and higher farther back, grew along the slopes of the hill on all sides. There was also some other bush that did not feel like sea grape, but Timothy did not know the name of it.

To the south, the beach sloped gradually out into the water. On the north side, it was different. There were submerged coral reefs and great shelves. The water became deep very abruptly. Timothy warned me against going into the water here because the sharks could swim close to the shore.

Timothy said that the water all around the cay was clear and that he could see all kinds of beautiful fish. There was brain coral and organ-pipe coral that the parrot fish would nibble.

From what I could feel and hear, our cay seemed a

lovely island and I wished that I could see it. I planned to walk around it at least once a day, following the vine rope from the ridge to the beach, then setting out along the sand.

I was starting to be less dependent on the vine rope, and sometimes it seemed to me that Timothy was trying hard to make me independent of him. I thought I knew why, but I did not talk to him about it. I did not want to think about the possibility of Timothy dying and leaving me alone on the cay.

Because the rain the night before had made us hopeful, I think both of us did our chores with one ear to the sky, listening for the sound of engines. But all day we heard nothing but familiar sounds, the surf, the wind and the cries of sea birds.

That night after dinner, Timothy grumbled, "No aircraft! D'islan' mus' 'ave a jumbi."

"Don't talk nonsense, Timothy," I said.

"D'evil spirit harass an' meliss us," he said darkly. "An' we do not 'ave a chicken or grains o' corn to chase 'im."

I said, "Timothy, you can't really believe in that."

My father had told me about "obediah", or "voodoo", in the West Indies. It had come over from Africa, of course. Haiti was the worst of all for it, but there was some practice on all the islands. It was mixed up with religion and witch doctors.

I knew he was looking at Stew Cat when he said, "Mebbe dat outrageous cat is d'jumbi."

"He's just an old cat, Timothy," I protested.

Recalling everything that had happened, Timothy said, "He came board d'raff, an' we got separated from all else; den d'young bahss' eyes got dark, gibbin' us exceedin' trouble; den we float up dis hombuggin' Debil's

Mout' . . ."

Angrily, I said, "Timothy, Stew Cat is not a jumbi. You leave him alone."

The old man was silent, and I was suddenly worried for Stew Cat's safety. Timothy stayed by me all night, but in the morning, when I awakened, he was gone and so was Stew Cat.

I crawled out of the hut and began to call for Stew. Then I called for Timothy. There was no answer. I went down the hill and headed up the beach towards the reef. Voodoo was silly, I knew, but it was also frightening. I couldn't understand why Timothy thought Stew Cat was the jumbi.

I decided to circle the island to find them. Using my cane to feel the way, to touch driftwood or coral ledges the night tide might have uncovered, I moved along the damp sand, calling out now and then.

When I reached the north side, Timothy answered, "Marnin', Phill-eep."

I asked him where he'd been.

He laughed. "Dere is lil' place to go 'ere. I 'ave been 'ere on dis beach."

"Where is Stew Cat?"

Timothy was silent.

I asked again.

"B'gettin' his own self a lizzard, mebbe, mebbe," he answered, but there was something conniving in his voice.

All the while, I could hear a scraping noise and, occasionally, a ring of metal. "What are you doing?" I asked.

"Cuttin' on an ol' piece o' wood," he replied.

Why would he be down on north beach this early cutting wood? I knew we had plenty for the campfire and the signal fire.

"And you haven't seen Stew Cat?"

"Not a 'air," he said.

I wanted to see what he had in his hands, but I didn't have the courage to walk up and touch it. I said, "Timothy, I'm very hungry."

I felt his hand on my wrist. He said, "We'll go to d'hut."

He made breakfast, we ate, and then without a word, he slipped away.

Usually, he kept his hunting knife in the tin box that had stored our biscuits. Also in that box were the dry matches we had left, a few pieces of stale chocolate and small things that Timothy had salvaged from the beach or the raft.

I felt a few nails, the hinges that had been on the raft's trap door, some short lengths of rope, a piece of cork, several small tin cans and a small roll of something that felt like leather. Nothing was missing except the knife, and I knew he'd taken it to north beach with him.

As best I could, I searched around the hut area for Stew Cat, thinking that maybe Timothy had tied him up somewhere. Yet I was certain he'd be miaowing if he was within hearing distance.

I was positive that Timothy was back on north beach cutting on that piece of wood, but something told me not to go down there. So I sat by the hut wondering what to do. It was no good trying to convince him that jumbi did not exist, nor was there any way to find Stew Cat if Timothy had hidden him.

The morning hours passed slowly. Once, I went down to east beach to sit near the signal fire, hoping to hear the drone of an aircraft. Several times, over the stir of the wind, I thought I heard a faint miaow, but I couldn't locate the direction.

Maybe all that had happened was beginning to work on the old man's mind. Maybe I was stranded on a tiny, forgotten island in the Caribbean with a madman. If he harmed Stew Cat because of some silly jumbi thing, I knew he might also harm me.

I thought about getting back on the raft and letting it drift to sea again. I was certain that there were enough boards still on top to sit and sleep on. If I could get the water keg down the hill, and the last pieces of chocolate out of the box, I'd be all right for a few days.

I got up and went down to the water, feeling my way towards the reef. I knew that if I kept going that way, I'd touch or fall over the length of life-line rope that tethered the raft. Timothy had driven a heavy piece of driftwood into the sand so that the raft would not go out to sea with the movement of the tide.

I walked slowly and carefully, expecting at any moment to feel the rope with my cane, or have it hit against my ankles. I went all the way to the beginning of the reef without finding it. Then I reversed my course and walked in the other direction. Finally, I stumbled over the heavy piece of wood that Timothy had driven into the sand.

I felt around it, but the rope was no longer tied to it. He'd cut the raft loose! Panic swept over me. But taking my bearing from the stake, I decided to go out into the water, hoping to find the raft.

A metre offshore, I got another bad scare. I put my foot down and something moved. In fact the whole bottom seemed to move. I lost my balance and fell headfirst into the water. I came up sputtering and realized I'd stepped on a skate, that diamond-shaped fish with a stinging tail. I'd done that once or twice at Westpunt. The skate is kin to the deadly sea ray, but this one was as shocked as I was and swam off to deep water.

I went out to my waist, feeling with my hands in all directions, but the raft was gone!

I trusted Timothy and kept telling myself that he wouldn't harm me, but it was the whole mysterious jumbi thing that was frightening. And he certainly wasn't acting like the Timothy I'd been living with.

In mid-afternoon he returned to the hut. Neither of us spoke.

Then I heard him pounding something. The palm fronds on the hut rattled; whatever it was, he was pounding it into the hut. Having finished, he went away again.

When I heard him moving through the sea grape down the path, I got up and began feeling around the framing of the hut. There was nothing on the sides of it, and I decided that whatever he'd attached had to be on the roof.

I knew there were several lengths of log over near the campfire. So I approached it, found one of the logs and rolled it over to the entrance to the hut. I stood on it and felt along the crossframe that held the roof up.

In the very centre I found what I was looking for. I cried out when the palm of my hand touched something sharp. Then with my fingers, I slowly felt around the object. It had a head, I discovered, four feet and a tail.

Timothy had spent all that time carving a cat, a Stew Cat. The nails in it were supposed to kill the evil jumbi.

I felt weak and sat down on the log.

Soon, he came up the path, dropping Stew Cat into my lap.

"Where was he?" I asked.

"On d'raff, o'course," Timothy answered. "I got 'im off d'islan' till I could chase d'jumbi."

"Where is the raft, Timothy?"

"'Twas off d'shore, Phill-eep. 'Tis back now. An' our luck is change."

But it didn't change. It got worse.

One morning in the middle of May, I awakened to hear

Timothy taking great breaths. It sounded as though he were fighting for air. I listened a moment and then asked, "Are you all right, Timothy?"

He wheezed back, "Feber! Malar!"

I had to think a moment to understand what he was talking about. Fever! Malaria! I reached over to touch him. His forehead was burning hot.

His breath coming in big, harsh sighs, he said, "I got malar agin, Phill-eep. 'Twill go away, but fetch some wattah."

When I had had fever in Virginia, and at Scharloo, my mother had given me aspirin and then put cold cloths on my head. But we had no aspirin on the cay, of course, and the water was always warm. I poured some water from the keg, and gave it to him. He gulped it and then fell back onto the palm mat.

For a while, I listened to his heavy breathing and then ripped a piece of cloth from what was left of my shirt, dampened it with water and placed it on his forehead. He murmured, "Dat be good," but suddenly he began to shiver, even though the morning air was already warm. I could hear his teeth chattering.

I had nothing to cover him with, so I just sat beside him holding the cloth, which was already beginning to dry, to his forehead. His breath was like air from a furnace.

It must have been about ten o'clock when Timothy began to mumble and laugh. It sounded almost as if he were talking in his sleep, but the laughter, little bursts of it between the wheezes, was very high and strange. I couldn't keep the cloth on his head because he was tossing from side to side.

I talked to him constantly, but he didn't even seem to know I was there.

Once he got up but fell back onto the mat, and I

told him to stay very still. For a long time he did, because he began to shiver again. When that ended, the mumbling and high laughter started all over again.

At about noon the mumbling got worse, and I could feel him trying to get to his feet. I clung to his arm, shouting for him to lie down again, but he threw me aside as if I weren't there. I could hear him crashing down the hill towards the sea, the frightening laughter echoing back.

I followed the trail of laughter. Then I heard splashing and knew he'd gone into the water. I yelled, "Timothy, Timothy, come back."

Suddenly it became dead quiet. I screamed his name again and again. There was no answer.

I reached the beach and waded out to my knees, then began to move slowly along, trying to keep on a line with the beach. I had gone about thirty steps when I fell over Timothy's body, plunging down in the water.

Holding onto him with one hand, I got to my feet again. The upper part of his body was floating but I knew his feet were dragging on the bottom. I put my face against his mouth. Yes, he was still breathing.

I worked myself around to put both hands under his shoulders, but he was too heavy that way. Then I clasped my hands under his chin, and began to pull him out. He made strange sounds, but did not try to help me.

It took me what seemed like a long time to get Timothy out of the water and back up on the damp sand. He must have weighed over a hundred kilograms, and I could only move him two or three centimetres at a time.

I sat beside him for almost an hour in the hot sun while he rested quietly, his breathing not so harsh now. Then I realized he was shivering again. I knew I could not drag him up the slope to the shelter of the hut, so I tore off branches of sea grape and put them over his body. The grape leaves cut the rays of the sun.

I brought water down from the hut, raised his head and ordered him to drink it. With one hand, I found his lips and then guided the cup to his chin. He seemed to understand and gulped it down.

I stayed by him the rest of the long afternoon while he slept. When he awakened, it was early evening and had turned cool again. He was breathing easily now, and I knew that the fever had broken because his forehead was no longer hot.

Sitting up, he said weakly, "How did I get downg 'ere?"

I told him he'd run down the hill.

"Dat debil, d'fever," Timothy sighed.

I said, "You went into the water. You scared me, Timothy."

"Dat be true," he said. "My 'ead burn wid fire, an' I put it out."

I helped him to his feet, and we went up the hill together, Timothy leaning on me for support for the first time. He never really regained his strength.

It was in late May that I believe Timothy decided we might stay there for ever. We had not seen a schooner sail nor heard an aeroplane since setting foot on the island.

I know it was late May because each day he dropped a small pebble into an old can that he'd found on the beach. It was our only way to tell how many days we'd been there. Every so often I'd count them, beginning with 9 April. We now had forty-eight pebbles in the can.

On this day, Timothy said thoughtfully, "Phill-eep, 'as it evah come into your own self that I might be poorly again some marnin'?" I knew he was thinking about malaria and the fever.

I said it had.

He said, "Well, you mus' den know how to provite your own self wid feesh."

For more than a week, I knew he had been labouring over nails to turn them into fish hooks. He always speared the fish or langosta with a sharp stick, but I could not see, of course, to do that. I knew he was making the hooks for me.

He said, with a secret tone in his voice, "I 'ave foun' an outrageous good 'ole on d'reef in a safe place."

We went down the hill and started out along the reef shelf. By now, my feet were tough and I hardly felt the jagged edges of the coral. But I knew that lurking in the tide pools were the treacherous sea urchins. Stepping on them invited a sharp spine in your foot, and Timothy had already warned me that, "dey veree poison, dey b'gibbin' you terrible pain."

Every metre, Timothy had driven a piece of driftwood deep into the coral crevices so that I could feel them as I went along. Neither of us knew what to do about the sea urchins, but Timothy said he'd think mightily about them. He had taken a large rock to smash them all along the path over the reef top. But in time they could come back.

We went out about fifteen metres along the reef, and then he said, "Now, we feesh."

He described the hole to me. It was about six metres in diameter and two and a half metres deep. The bottom was sandy, but mostly free of coral so that my hooks would not snag. He said there was a "mos' natural" opening to the sea, so that the fish could swim in and out of this coral-walled pool.

He took my hand to have me feel all around the edges of the hole. The coral had been smoothed over by centuries of sea wash. Timothy said that the sand in the sea water acted like a grindstone on the sharp edges of the coral. It was not completely smooth but there were no jagged edges sticking out.

"Now, reach downg 'ere," Timothy said, "an' tug off d'mussel."

I put my hand into the warm water, kneeling down over the ledge, and felt a mussel. But in ripping it loose, I lost my balance and only Timothy's hand prevented me from falling in. If you are blind, the sensation of falling can be terrifying. My memory of the fall off the raft was still very clear.

Timothy said, "Easy dere, Phill-eep. Jus' sit a moment an' relax."

His voice was soothing. "If evah you do fall, jus' stay in d'hole awhile, feel which way d'wattah washes, den follow it to d'ledge, grab hol' an' pull your own self out."

Timothy guided my hands in opening the tough mussel shell and digging the slippery meat out to bait the hook.

"'Tis an outrageous sharp knife, so be veree careful o' your fingers."

Then he told me to feel the hook and slip the mussel bait over the barb. I'd fished many times with my father and this was easy.

Rusty bolts served as sinkers. Timothy had found several pieces of wood with bolts in them, had burned them, then raked the bolts out of the ashes. He'd unravelled a life line from the raft to make single strands for the fishing line.

I dropped the hook and sinker overboard. In a moment there was a sharp tug. I jerked, flipping the fish back over my shoulder so it would land on the reef. Timothy cheered and told me to feel along the line to the wriggling fish, then take the hook out.

Squirming and jumping in my hand, it was small but fat. I grinned over towards Timothy. When I had fished before this, it was fun. Now I felt I had done something very special. I was learning to do things all over again, by touch and feel.

I said to Timothy, "Dis is outrageous, hombuggin' good feesh 'ole."

He laughed with pleasure.

Every day after that I did all the fishing. Timothy, of course, continued to get langosta. He had to dive for them, but I caught all the fish. After the third morning, he let me go out alone on the reef. I'd feel my way along his driftwood posts, find the hole, pry a mussel loose and then fish.

I was alone on the reef but somehow I always felt he was sitting on the beach nearby. I could sense his presence, yet he was always at the hut when I got back there.

We often talked about the cay and what was on it. Timothy had not thought much about it. He took it for granted that the cay was always there, but I told him about geography, and how maybe a volcano could have caused the Devil's Mouth. He'd listen in fascination, almost speechless.

We talked about how the little coral animals might have been building the foundations of the cay for thousands of years. I said, "Then sand began to gather on it, and after a few more years it was finally an island."

It was as if a new world had opened up for Timothy. He kept using that same expression, "Dat be true?"

I found out that he'd never thought about how the sea grape, or the vines, or the coconuts came to our cay. I told him what I knew.

Seeds had drifted in from the sea, or birds had brought them. After a rain, they'd taken root.

"D'lizzard?" he asked sternly.

"I'd bet a bird, flying from another island, holding a mother lizard in its beak, dropped it here. Then the baby lizards were born. Or maybe a mother lizard washed ashore on driftwood during a storm."

Timothy was very impressed, and I felt good that I'd been able to tell him something.

We found a lot to talk about.

I think it was the fifth afternoon of this week that I blurted out to Timothy, "I'll climb the palm now."

"Eh, Phill-eep," he said, and I could almost see the grin on his face and the light in his eyes as he looked skywards. Greedily, I'm sure.

He said, "Dere is one coconut tree ovah dere dat 'as a sway in 'is back like an ol' horse. Dat is d'one to clim'."

I was trembling a little as he led me to the tree, telling me I should go up just a short way; climb it like a monkey. If I could do it, I was to come back down, put the knife between my teeth and go up again.

The trunk of this palm tree must have been about a metre in diameter because I could easily put my hands around to the back. I grasped it, hunched my body, placed my bare feet on the rough trunk and began to climb. Timothy was probably holding his breath.

I went up about three metres and froze. I could not move up or down. My legs and arms were rigid.

Timothy, standing below to catch me if I fell, called up softly, "Phill-eep, 'tis no shame to ease your own self back downg to d'san'."

Slowly I began to back down along the trunk. The bark was rough against my hands and feet, but what I felt most was Timothy's disappointment. I couldn't have been more than a metre off the ground when I took a deep breath and said to myself, if you fall, you'll fall in sand.

Then I started climbing again.

Timothy called up, "You 'ave forgot d'knife."

I knew that if I stopped now, I'd never climb it. I didn't answer him but kept my hands and feet moving steadily. Then I heard him shout, "You b'gettin' to d'top." Palm fronds brushed my head. I grasped the base of one to pull myself up. Timothy let out a roar of joy.

Then he told me how to reach the coconuts. It took a long time to pull, tug and twist two of them loose. But they finally fell. I stayed in the palm for another few minutes to rest, then slid down. I had won.

As my feet touched the ground, Timothy hugged me, yelling, "D'palm harass us no more."

We drank every drop of the coconut milk, and feasted on the fresh meat.

Squatting near me, his teeth crunching the coconut, Timothy said, "You see, Phill-eep, you do not need d'eye now. You 'ave done widout d'eye what I couldn't do wid my whole body."

It was almost as if I'd graduated from the survival course that Timothy had been putting me through since we had landed on the cay.

It rained that night, a very soft rain. Not even enough to drip through the palm-frond roof. Timothy breathed softly beside me. I had now been with him every moment of the day and night for two months, but I had not seen him. I remembered his face. But now, in my memory, it did not seem strange at all. It seemed only kind and strong.

I asked, "Timothy, are you still black?"

His laughter filled the hut.

Theodore Taylor

More than a century ago, the Indian inhabitants of an island off the coast of California were removed from their island home. One young woman was, for some reason, left behind. She lived for eighteen years on the island where the only other inhabitants were wild dogs. Those are the historical facts on which this story is based.

Island of the Blue Dolphins

There had been wild dogs on the Island of the Blue Dolphins as long as I can remember, but after the Aleuts had slain most of the men of our tribe and their dogs had left to join the others, the pack became much bolder. It spent the nights running through the village and during the day was never far off. It was then that we made plans to get rid of them, but the ship came and everyone left Ghalas-at.

I am sure that the pack grew bolder because of their leader, the big one with the thick fur round his neck and the yellow eyes.

I had never seen this dog before the Aleuts came and no one else

had, so he must have come with them and been left behind when they sailed away. He was a much larger dog than any of ours, which besides have short hair and brown eyes. I was sure that he was an Aleut dog.

Already I had killed four of the pack, but there were many left, more than in the beginning, for some had been born in the meantime. The young dogs were even wilder than the old ones.

I first went to the hill near the cave when the pack was away and collected armfuls of brush which I placed near the mouth of their lair. Then I waited until the pack was in the cave. The dogs went there early in the morning to sleep after they had spent the night prowling. I took with me the big bow and five arrows and two of the spears. I went quietly, circling the mouth of the cave and came up to it from the side. There I left all of my weapons except one spear.

I set fire to the brush and pushed it into the cave. If the wild dogs heard me, there was no sound from them. Nearby was a ledge of rock which I climbed, taking my weapons with me.

The fire burned high. Some of the smoke trailed out over the hill, but much of it stayed in the cave. Soon the pack would have to leave. I did not hope to kill more than five of them because I had only that many arrows, but if the leader was one of the five I would be satisfied. It might be wiser if I waited and saved all my arrows for him, and this I decided to do.

None of the dogs appeared before the fire died. Then three ran out and away. Seven more followed and a long time afterwards a like number. There were many more still left in the cave.

The leader came next. Unlike the others, he did not run away. He jumped over the ashes and stood at the mouth of the cave, sniffing the air. I was so close to him that I could see his nose quivering, but he did not see me until I raised my bow. Fortunately I did not frighten him.

He stood facing me, his front legs spread as if he were ready to spring, his yellow eyes narrowed to slits. The arrow struck him in the chest. He turned away from me, took one step and fell. I sent another arrow towards him which went wide.

At this time three more dogs trotted out of the cave. I used the last of my arrows and killed two of them.

Carrying both of the spears, I climbed down from the ledge and went through the brush to the place where the leader had fallen. He was not there. While I had been shooting at the other dogs, he had gone. He could not have gone far because of his wound, but though I looked everywhere, around the ledge where I had been standing and in front of the cave, I did not find him.

I waited for a long time and then went inside the cave. It was deep, but I could see clearly.

Far back in a corner was the half-eaten carcass of a fox. Beside it was a black dog with four grey pups. One of the pups came slowly towards me, a round ball of fur that I could have held in my hand. I wanted to hold it, but the mother leaped to her feet and bared her teeth. I raised my spear as I backed out of the cave, yet I

did not use it. The wounded leader was not there.

Night was coming and I left the cave, going along the foot of the hill that led to the cliff. I had not gone far on this trail that the wild dogs used when I saw the broken shaft of an arrow. It had been gnawed off near the tip and I knew it was from the arrow that had wounded the leader.

Farther on I saw his tracks in the dust. They were uneven as if he were travelling slowly. I followed them towards the cliff, but finally lost them in the darkness.

The next day and the next it rained and I did not go to look for him. I spent those days making more arrows, and on the third day, with these arrows and my spear, I went out along the trail the wild dogs had made to and from my house.

There were no tracks after the rain, but I followed the trail to the pile of rocks where I had seen them before. On the far side of the rocks I found the big grey dog. He had the broken arrow in his chest and he was lying with one of his legs under him.

He was about ten paces from me so I could see him clearly. I was sure that he was dead, but I lifted the spear and took a good aim at him. Just as I was about to throw the spear, he raised his head a little from the earth and then let it drop.

This surprised me greatly and I stood there for a while not knowing what to do, whether to use the spear or my bow. I was used to animals playing dead until they suddenly turned on you or ran away.

The spear was the better of the two weapons at this distance, but I could not use it as well as the other, so I climbed onto the rocks where I could see him if he ran. I placed my feet carefully. I had a second arrow ready should I need it. I fitted an arrow and pulled back the string, aiming at his head.

Why I did not send the arrow I cannot say. I stood on the rock with the bow pulled back and my hand would not let it go. The big dog lay there and did not move and this may have been the reason. If he had got up I would have killed him. I stood there for a long time looking down at him and then I climbed off the rocks.

He did not move when I went up to him, nor could I see him breathing until I was very close. The head of the arrow was in his chest and the broken shaft was covered with blood. The thick fur round his neck was matted from the rain.

I do not think that he knew I was picking him up, for his body was limp, as if he were dead. He was very heavy and the only way I could lift him was by kneeling and putting his legs round my shoulders.

In this manner, stopping to rest when I was tired, I carried him to the headland.

I could not get through the opening under the fence, so I cut the bindings and lifted out two of the whale ribs and thus took him into the house. He did not look at me or raise his head when I laid him on the floor, but his mouth was open and he was breathing.

The arrow had a small point, which was fortunate, and came out easily though it had gone deep. He did not move while I did this, nor afterwards as I cleaned the wound with a peeled stick from a coral bush. This bush has poisonous berries, yet its wood often heals wounds that nothing else will.

I had not gathered food for many days and the baskets were empty, so I left water for the dog and, after mending the fence, went down to the sea. I had no thought that he would live and I did not care.

All day I was among the rocks gathering shellfish and only once did I think of the wounded dog, my enemy, lying there in the house, and then to wonder why I had not killed him.

He was still alive when I got back, though he had not moved from the place where I had left him. Again I cleaned the wound with a coral twig. I then lifted his head and put water into his mouth, which he swallowed. This was the first time that he had looked at me since the time I had found him on the trail. His eyes were sunken and they

looked out at me from far back in his head.

Before I went to sleep I gave him more water. In the morning I left food for him when I went down to the sea, and when I came home he had eaten it. He was lying in the corner, watching me. While I made a fire and cooked my supper, he watched me. His yellow eyes followed me wherever I moved.

That night I slept on the rock, for I was afraid of him, and at dawn as I went out, I left the hole under the fence open so he could go. But he was there when I got back, lying in the sun with his head on his paws. I had speared two fish, which I cooked for my supper. Since he was very thin, I gave him one of them, and after he had eaten it he came over and lay down by the fire, watching me with his yellow eyes that were very narrow and slanted up at the corners.

For four nights I slept on the rock, and every morning I left the hole under the fence open so that he could leave. Each day I speared a fish for him and when I got home he was always at the fence waiting for it. He would not take the fish from me so I had to put it on the ground. Once I held out my hand to him, but at this he backed away and showed his teeth.

On the fourth day when I came back from the rocks early he was not there at the fence waiting. A strange feeling came over me. Always before when I returned, I had hoped that he would be gone. But now as I crawled under the fence I did not feel the same.

I called out, "Dog, Dog," for I had no other name for him.

I ran towards the house, calling it. He was inside. He was just getting to his feet, stretching himself and yawning. He looked first at the fish I carried and then at me and moved his tail.

That night I stayed in the house. Before I fell asleep I thought of a name for him, for I could not call him Dog. The name I thought of was Rontu, which means in our language, Fox Eyes.

Scott O'Dell

Scott O'Dell's story is based on the true experience of an Indian woman stranded on San Nicolas Island in the 1800s. George Nidever was one of those who actually found this woman after her years of solitude.

The Lone Woman of San Nicolas Island

The next morning we had breakfast early. Then all hands but the cook went on shore, at the same place where we had landed the day before. We decided to search first from about the middle of the island up towards the head. The four men struck across the low sandy stretch, and found the basket and its contents carefully replaced in the crook of the bush in which we had first discovered it. Charley and I struck up towards the head of the island. Reaching the place where he had seen the footprints the day before, he followed up the ridge. Near its top he found several huts made of whale's ribs and covered with brush. It was so long since they had been occupied that they were open on all sides and the grass was quite high within. Looking about in all directions from this point, he discovered at a distance, along the ridge, a small black object about the size of a crow. Advancing cautiously towards it he soon discovered it to be the Indian woman. Only her head and shoulders were visible above one of the small huts resembling those we had before discovered. He approached as near as he dared. Then, raising his hat on his ramrod, he signalled to the men who were then recrossing the low sandy stretch, and were plainly visible from this point.

They saw the signals, and came towards him. In the meantime, the old woman was stripping the blubber from a piece of seal skin. She held it across one knee, using in the operation a rude knife made from a piece of iron hoop stuck into a piece of rough wood for a handle. She kept up a continual jabbering to herself and every few moments would stop and look in the direction of our men. She had evidently been watching them, her hand placed over her eyes to shade them from the sun.

Upon his first approach there were some dogs near, which began to growl. These the old woman sent away with a yell but without looking in the direction of Charley. The men having come up, they quietly surrounded her to prevent any attempt at escape.

This being done, Charley stepped around in front of her. Instead of showing any alarm, she smiled and bowed, chattering away to them in a language wholly unintelligible to all of them, even to the Indians. They seated themselves around her, after having made signs to me to come up. I at first did not care to go. I supposed that they had simply discovered something that excited their curiosity and I would hear about it when they should come down. They continued to make signs to me to come there, however, so I went up and found them seated around the old woman. She smiled and bowed to me also. Having taken a seat she took some roots of two different kinds, one called *corcomites* and the name of the other I do not know. She placed them in the fire which was burning within the hut. As soon as they were roasted she invited us all to eat some.

The site of the hut where we found her was on the north-west side and near the top of the ridge that forms the upper end of the

island. It was not far from the best springs of water, near to the best point for fish and seal, and it commanded a good view of the greater portion of the island. Just outside the hut or wind break, as I should call it, was a large pile of ashes and another of bones. This must have been her abode for a long time. Nearby were several stakes with blubber on them, as we had seen around the other huts. There was blubber also hanging on a sinew rope which was stretched between two stakes. Near the hut were several baskets, some in the process of construction, also two bottle-shaped vessels for holding water. These, as well as the baskets, were woven, and of some species of grass very common on the island. There were also several other articles: fish-hooks made of bone, and needles of the same material, lines or cords of sinews for fishing and the larger rope of sinews she no doubt used for snaring seals on the rocks where they came to sleep.

The old woman was of medium height, but rather thick. She must have been about fifty years old, but she was still strong and active. Her face was pleasing, as she was continually smiling. Her teeth were entire but worn to the gums, the effect, no doubt, of eating the dried seal blubber. Her head, which had evidently been for years without any protection, was covered with thick matted hair. It was once black, no doubt, but now it had become a dull brown colour. Her clothing consisted of but a single garment made in the form of a gown. It fitted close at the neck, had no sleeves, was girded at the waist with a sinew cord and reached nearly to the feet. She had another dress of the same material and make in one of the baskets. These were sewn with sinews, the needles used being of bone. This place was undoubtedly where she usually lived, but in the rainy season she lived in a cave nearby.

Having been requested by the Fathers at the Mission of Santa Barbara to bring her off if we found her, I asked the Indians if they thought that she could be taken by force if necessary. They thought she could. Charley Brown was of the opinion that no force would be necessary in taking her. I thereupon made signs to her to go with us, but she stared at me seemingly without comprehending what was wanted. Charley then placed his hand on her shoulder to call her attention. Then he went through the motions of putting her things in baskets and then these on his back, at the conclusion of which he said vamoose. This she understood without any difficulty, for she

at once began putting her things into her baskets.

Her basket filled, she put it on her back and followed the Indians towards the beach while we walked behind, each of us carrying some of her things. Seal meat, some of it stinking, and a seal's head from which putrefied brains were running, were all carefully put into the basket. We soon arrived at a spring of water where we stopped. On some stakes which we found standing nearby we hung the things we were carrying, fixing them onto the stakes in such a manner as to lead her to believe we took very great care of them. Near this spring there were several rocks. In the cracks of these rocks were large numbers of fish and other bones, carefully placed. We then proceeded to the beach, where a spring issues from a rock, just below the bank. The old woman stopped here to wash. The men went on ahead and Charley and I remained on the bank above. This being finished, we proceeded to the boat and went on board the schooner.

When we put her into the boat, she crept forward to the bow where she knelt, holding firmly on to either side. As soon as we got on board the schooner, she crept alongside the stove which was on deck. Dinner was ready and was at once served. The cook gave the old woman some pork and hard tack, which she seemed to relish. In fact she took readily to all of our food, it always agreeing with her. Charley Brown at once set to work and made her a petticoat of ticking, which, with a man's cotton shirt and a black tie, he completed her dress. She seemed to be very proud of it. Seeing Charley at work on her petticoat, she made signs that she wanted to sew. Accordingly, she was given a needle and thread, but Charley was obliged to thread it for her as her eyes seemed weak.

I had given her an old cloak or cape that was almost in ribbons and she sewed up all the rents and holes. Her manner of sewing was peculiar. Placing her work across her knee she thrust the needle through the cloth with the right hand and pulled the thread taut with the left. The next day we went ashore and camped, about the middle of the island, close to the beach. We made a temporary shelter by spreading a sail over two oars driven into the side of the bank. A similar shelter of brush was made for her.

We remained here hunting for about a month, when we brought her on shore with us. While on the island with us, she busied herself in going for wood and water and working on her baskets. She brought water and wood of her own accord, and water in the vessels before mentioned.

Of the several baskets she was working on, not one of them was completed, although she would work first on one, then on the other. One day Charley shot a she otter offshore. It was brought to land for the purpose of skinning it. The carcass was being hauled down to the water, as was customary after taking off the skin, when the old woman vigorously protested against such a waste of meat. Seizing one of the flippers she drew it back on land, where it lay until the stench obliged us to throw it in the water. By this time, however, she had come to the conclusion that our food was better than this. She expressed this in her own rude way by signs. She was very fond of sugar, and in fact anything sweet, and showed her fondness for it by smacking her lips. She had evidently known hunger as she saved every scrap of food and bones. The latter she would take out from time to time, suck them over and over, and then put them away again.

When we took her from her hut, she was very careful to place the seal's head in the basket although it was almost rotten. One day, while out hunting, I came across her lining one of the vessels she used for holding water. She had built a fire and had several small stones about the size of a walnut heating in it. Taking one of the vessels, she dropped a few pieces of asphalt within it, and as soon as the stones were well heated they were dropped in on top of the asphalt. They soon melted it. Then resting the bottom of the vessel on the ground, she gave it a rotary motion with both hands until its interior was completely covered with asphalt. These vessels hold water well, and if kept full may be placed with safety in a hot sun.

When we left the island for Santa Barbara, we were caught in such a violent gale that we were several times on the point of turning back. We finally got under the lee of Santa Cruz Island, which afforded us some shelter until late in the day when the wind went down. As soon as it began to blow, the old woman conveyed to us by signs her intention to stop the wind. She then knelt and prayed, facing the quarter from which the wind blowed. She continued to pray at intervals during the day until the gale was over. Then she looked at us and smiled as much as to say, "You see how I have succeeded in stopping the wind."

From Santa Cruz we ran over to Santa Barbara, arriving there early the next day. Upon nearing the shore an ox-cart came into sight. The old woman's delight was unbounded. She clapped her hands and danced, pointing at the cart and oxen. On landing I found my sons at the beach awaiting my arrival, one of them being on horseback.

Her delight at the sight of the horse was even greater than at the sight of the ox-cart. As soon as she got out of the boat, she went up to it and began examining it, pointing at this part, then that, and talking and laughing to herself. Finally she pointed at the horse and placing two fingers of her right hand astride the forefinger of her left, she imitated the motion of a horse. The news of the arrival of the old woman was not long in spreading. We had barely reached my house with her when half of the town came down to see her.

For weeks after, she and her things—her dress, baskets, needle,

etc.—were visited by everybody in the town and for many kilometres around it.

The old woman was always in a good humour. She sang and danced, to the great delight of the children and even the older ones. She often visited the town and seldom returned without some present. The vessels that touched here usually brought passengers who, hearing of her, came to my house. The Captain of the *Fremont*, one of these vessels, offered to take her to San Francisco and exhibit her, giving me one half of what he could make. Captain Trussel of this place offered me a thousand dollars for her for the same purpose. We had all become somewhat attached to her, so we refused to listen to these proposals.

The same day that we arrived here, the Fathers from the Mission came down to see her. They continued to visit her. They sent for Indians from different parts of this area, who spoke different Indian tongues, in the hopes of finding someone who could converse with her. Several came, each representing a different dialect, but none of them could understand her or make themselves understood. She was continually talking and frequently made use of the *piccaninny* in referring to her child. She also used *mañana*. She expressed a great many ideas by signs, so plainly that we readily understood them. By signs she told us that she did not find her child, that she wandered about for days without tasting any food or drink, sometimes sleeping but little, until her clothes were torn, and her feet and legs bleeding.

After a time she forgot her child and sang and danced. She also told us that she was very sick at one time; that she had seen vessels passing to and fro but none came to take her off; that she saw us on the island before we found her.

About five weeks after she was brought over, she was taken sick from eating too much fruit, and seven weeks from the day of her arrival she died.

George Nidever

That There Dog O'Mine

Macquarie the shearer had met with an accident. To tell the truth, he had been in a drunken row at a wayside shanty, from which he had escaped with three fractured ribs, a cracked head, and various minor abrasions. His dog, Tally, had been a sober but savage participator in the drunken row, and had escaped with a broken leg. Macquarie afterwards shouldered his swag and staggered and struggled along the track sixteen kilometres to the Union Town Hospital. Lord knows how he did it. He didn't exactly know himself. Tally limped behind all the way, on three legs.

The doctors examined the man's injuries and were surprised at his endurance. Even doctors are surprised sometimes—though they don't always show it. Of course, they would take him in, but they objected to Tally. Dogs were not allowed on the premises.

"You will have to turn that dog out," they said to the shearer, as he sat on the edge of a bed.

Macquarie said nothing.

"We cannot allow dogs about the place, my man," said the doctor in a louder tone, thinking the man was deaf.

"Tie him up in the yard, then."

"No. He must go out. Dogs are not permitted on the grounds."

Macquarie rose slowly to his feet, shut his agony behind his set teeth, painfully buttoned his shirt over his hairy chest, took up his waistcoat and staggered to the corner where the swag lay.

"What are you going to do?" they asked.

"You ain't going to let my dog stop?"

"No. It's against the rules. There are no dogs allowed on the premises."

He stooped and lifted his swag, but the pain was too great, and he leaned back against the wall.

"Come, come now! man alive!" exclaimed the doctor, impatiently. "You must be mad. You know you are not in a fit state to go out. Let the wardsman help you to undress."

"No!" said Macquarie. "No. If you won't take my dog in you don't take me. He's got a broken leg and wants fixing up just—just as much as—as I do. If I'm good enough to come in, he's good enough—and—and better."

He paused a while, breathing painfully, and then went on.

"That—that there old dog of mine has follered me faithful and true, these twelve long hard and hungry years. He's about—about the only thing that ever cared whether I lived or fell and rotted on the cursed track."

He rested again; then he continued: "That—that there dog was pupped on the track," he said, with a sad sort of a smile. "I carried him for months in a billy, and afterwards on my swag when he knocked up. . . . And the old slut—his mother—she'd foller along quite contented —and sniff the billy now and again—just to see if he was all right. . . . She follered me for God knows how many years. She follered me till she was blind—and for a year after. She follered me till she could crawl along through the dust no longer—and—and then I killed her, because I couldn't leave her behind alive!"

He rested again.

"And this here old dog," he continued, touching Tally's upturned nose with his knotted fingers, "this here old dog has follered me for—for ten years; through floods and droughts, through fair times and—and hard—mostly hard; and kept me from going mad when I had no mate nor money on the lonely track; and watched over me for weeks when I was drunk—drugged and poisoned at the cursed shanties; and saved my life more'n once, and got

kicks and curses very often for thanks; and forgave me for it all; and—and fought for me. He was the only living thing that stood up for me against that crawling pack of curs when they set onter me at the shanty back yonder—and he left his mark on some of 'em too; and—and so did I."

He took another pause.

Then he drew in his breath, shut his teeth hard, shouldered his swag, stepped into the doorway and faced round again.

The dog limped out of the corner and looked up anxiously.

"That there dog," said Macquarie to the hospital staff in general, "is a better dog than I'm a man—or you too, it seems—and a better Christian. He's been a better mate to me than I ever was to any man—or any man to me. He's watched over me; kep' me from getting robbed

many a time; fought for me; saved my life and took drunken kicks and curses for thanks—and forgave me. He's been a true, straight, honest and faithful mate to me—and I ain't going to desert him now. I ain't going to kick him out in the road with a broken leg. I—Oh, my God! my back!"

He groaned and lurched forwards, but they caught him, slipped off the swag and laid him on the bed.

Half an hour later the shearer was comfortably fixed up. "Where's my dog?" he asked, when he came to himself.

"Oh, the dog's all right," said the nurse, rather impatiently. "Don't bother. The doctor's setting his leg out in the yard."

Henry Lawson

Glossary

abode home or dwelling

abrasion *1* grazed or skinned place on the body *2* the act of rubbing or scraping off

artifact product of human art and workmanship, usually prehistoric

asphalt tarry mixture used to make a smooth hard surface on roads and paths

assign *1* to give to someone as his share or as his task *2* to decide upon

aurora the dawn

authoritative possessing authority, commanding; very reliable

bank *1* institution which receives and pays out money on behalf of its customers *2* to build up an earthen mound or barrier *3* to put an aircraft at an angle in turning to avoid sideslip *4* sides of river or lake

bats in the belfry crazy or eccentric

billy tin can used as a kettle when camping

bladder *1* thin bag of skin or rubber, etc. which is easily stretched by the liquid or air inside *2* bag-like inner part of the body that holds urine

bounty *1* a gift *2* generosity

broiled grilled

brush *1* instrument set with bristles, hairs, etc. used for cleaning, scrubbing or painting *2* broken or cut branches and twigs; a thicket *3* skirmish or encounter

calypso West Indian folk song telling about recent events (often made up by the singer as he goes along)

catacombs cemetery or galleries with recesses for tombs located under the surface of the earth

catchment something that catches water

causeway raised road or pathway (especially across water or marshy ground)

cay small island of coral or sand

commandeer to take; to seize

communal of a community; shared by many

compassion sorrow felt for another person; mercy

conniving *1* taking no notice or pretending ignorance of some wrong-doing *2* co-operating secretly or having secret agreement

constrict to press together tightly; to compress

convulsively with violent shaking movements

crevice crack or narrow opening

crook *1* curve, bend *2* staff with a hook at the end *3* dishonest person

cur *1* mongrel dog *2* mean, cowardly person

dialect way of speaking used in a particular part of a country, or by a particular group of people

doggedly persistently, stubbornly

fagged out (*slang*) weary; exhausted

flail *1* implement for threshing corn by hand *2* to strike with or as if with a flail; to thrash

frangipani red jasmine shrub

frigid *1* cold; frozen with cold *2* very cold and unfriendly in manner

futile useless; having no effect

gaff to seize (fish) with a barbed fishing spear

galvanize *1* to stimulate by an electric current; to rouse suddenly *2* to coat with zinc to prevent rusting

hankering yearning or longing for something

horny hard as horn; callous

imminent likely to happen very soon

immortality *1* deathlessness *2* undying fame

incredulously not believing, showing disbelief

infirmary hospital

kibbutz (*pl.* **kibbutzim**) farming centre in Israel which is shared by a group of people

kibbutznik one who lives and works on a kibbutz

lacerated torn; wounded

lemming small arctic gnawing animal (rather like a water rat)

lily-livered lacking courage; cowardly

lineage one's ancestry

manoeuvre to manage skilfully

meandering to flow in a winding course; to wander about without any particular destination

mission *1* group of people sent out to spread a particular religious belief *2* the purpose for which a messenger, delegate, etc. is sent out

monotonous *1* in one unchanging tone *2* dull

morass marsh; swamp

mullet type of small edible sea fish

orderly *1* soldier who carries the orders and messages of an officer *2* hospital attendant *3* in order; arranged

pacifyingly in an attempt to calm or bring peace to

parka skin jacket with hood attached, worn by Eskimos

pessimism the habit of thinking that things are likely to turn out badly

piccaninny child, especially of Negroes or South African or Australian natives

piling heavy beams driven vertically into bed of river, soft ground, etc. as support for bridge, dock, etc.

pinion to bind a person's arms or a bird's wings

precarious doubtful; uncertain

putrified rotten; decayed

quaver *1* to tremble or shake *2* (*in music*) to trill

radial arranged in rays, with parts extending in a straight line from a centre like the spokes of a wheel

ramrod *1* a rod for ramming down the charge into a muzzle-loading gun *2* a rod for cleaning a gun barrel

rancid smelling or tasting stale, bad or musty

rankle to cause annoyance or irritation

reeve to thread (rope, rod, etc.) through ring or other opening

relish to enjoy; to like the taste of

retrieve to recover anything lost; to regain

rotary turning like a wheel

rude *1* primitive; rough *2* ill-mannered, not polite

ruefully sorrowfully

scant barely sufficient; not plentiful

self-contempt scorn of oneself

serum *1* thin clear liquid forming part of the blood *2* dose of this fluid used to make another person or animal immune from a poison or disease

shamefaced *1* ashamed *2* very shy or bashful

shanty *1* roughly built hut; ramshackle dwelling *2* (or chanty) a sailor's worksong with chorus

simultaneously at the same time

skiff small light boat that can be rowed or sailed by one person

skua kind of gull-like sea bird which pursues other birds and makes them vomit the fish they have caught

snag *1* an unexpected problem or difficulty *2* sharp piece of a branch or stump left sticking out when the rest of the tree has been broken off

snuff out *1* to nip off the burnt portion of a candle or lamp wick *2* to extinguish or put out

squally strong and gusty

steel *1* to harden or strengthen one's courage *2* very strong metal made from iron hardened by the addition of a little carbon

sullen gloomy-looking; silent and angry

tack *1* food; fare *2* short nail with a broad flat head *3* to change sailing direction

tenaciously with a firm hold of; stubbornly, persistently

ticking heavy, usually stripped cotton or linen material, used for mattress covers

totem animal or plant taken by tribe, family group, etc. as symbol or emblem; an image of this

tundra level treeless plain in northern arctic regions

vamoose go quickly, be gone

vice *1* instrument for holding something tightly, by means of two metal jaws closed by a screw *2* bad habit

voodoo African witchcraft

weltering rolling about, wallowing; being washed about

white-out condition of the atmosphere, especially in polar regions, marked by dense snow-cloud hiding all physical features